Exposing the

Spirit

of

Self-Pity

1st Edition October 2011
2nd Edition January 2012
3rd Ediction March 2012

Written by: Caspar McCloud

Published by Life Application Ministries Publications (LAMP)
P.O. Box 165
Mt. Aukum, CA 95656
lamp@truthfrees.org

Editors: Joseph Lemmo and Gaynor Barradell

Permission is granted to use this material for teaching and
ministry purposes.

For copies: Please contact Caspar McCloud Ministries, Inc.

Printer: createspace.com

Index

Opening Prayer...4

Chapter One - Understanding the Spirit of Self-Pity 5

Chapter Two - Minions of Self-Pity...............................27

Chapter Three - The Mind of the Spirit of Self-Pity 48

Chapter Four - Blessings Come to Those Who Trust.....70

Chapter Five - The Fight for Our Lives 89

Chapter Six - Self-Pity and Relationships....................116

About the Author...136

What Others Have Said About Caspar 137

Internet Links 139

Live Video Links..140

Books Offered 141

Contact Information 142

Opening Prayer

Papa God I pray in the all powerful name of Jesus Christ of Nazareth Messiah Yeshua's name and I thank You now in advance that You will take all the words on the pages of this book to bless all those now who read it. And that Your supernatural peace will come and overtake them as they do. That You will guide and direct each person reading this book that they will find tremendous freedom in Your amazing mercy, grace and love.

As You have told us in the Holy Bible that If we continue in Your Word we will know the truth and the truth shall make us free. That those reading this would come to an acknowledging of the truth that they may recover themselves out of the snare of the devil, who has taken advantage of any lack of knowledge in certain areas of their life to try and make them prisoners. I thank You Lord that You will use this book to help free every captive who reads it. That as they find their freedom You will bless them and use them to help others find their freedom.

So I pray my Lord that You will cause the Holy Spirit to teach all those who read this book so that blessings and healing and restoration overtake them and chase them down in Jesus Christ of Nazareth Messiah Yeshua's name. Amen.

Your bond servant, Caspar McCloud

Chapter One

Understanding the Spirit of Self-pity

Over the years I have been called to minister, I have seen that if someone is entertaining a spirit of self-pity they cannot really get healed. So this spirit is a major factor in keeping a person sick and diseased. In other words, they are not able to get free from the curse which has cursed their health and the work of their hands. No matter what they try to do, they do not seem able to prosper and stay in the covenant relationships with the Lord.

They struggle with finances; they struggle with health and relationships. Because in the end that spirit of self-pity is protecting the spirit of Fear that God did not give you.

And we know that Fear has torment. 1 John 4:18 *There is no fear in love; but perfect love casteth out fear: because fear hath torment. He that feareth is not made perfect in love.*

When you are not loved properly, a spirit of self-pity can prevent you from being delivered from the spirit of fear because fear won't go unless we deal with the un-loving antichrist, luciferian, evil unclean spirit, which holds fear in place. Because a spirit of self-pity separates you from Papa God, yourself, and others.

One of the first places we find in dealing with self-pity is a broken heart which often is the result of a broken relationship with a father or mother or both. Your parents may have failed you in some way, but the Word of God tells us we still must give them honour simply because of who they are, or were.

Matthew 19:19 *Honour thy father and [thy] mother: and, Thou shalt love thy neighbour as thyself.*

Matthew 22:37-40 *Jesus said unto him, Thou shalt love the Lord thy God with all thy heart, and with all thy soul, and with all thy mind. This is the first and great commandment. And the second [is] like unto it, Thou shalt love thy neighbor as thyself. On these two commandments hang all the law and the prophets.*

For example, that spirit of self-pity is not keeping you in faith, and without faith it is absolutely impossible to please the Lord. Hebrews 11:6 *But without faith it is impossible to please him: for he that cometh to God must believe that he is, and that he is a rewarder of them that diligently seek him.*

How will you diligently seek the Lord if you are entertaining self-pity, and how can you stay in faith when you are not trusting Him? Every single thought we have must travel a pathway of faith or fear. We get to choose if we will obey the Lord and stay in Faith or we will obey the lies of the devil and go into fear.

I believe that a spirit of self-pity can actually stop the blessings of the Lord from reaching you, which seems most often the case, except when He chooses to have mercy. Romans 9:15 *For he saith to Moses, I will have mercy on whom I will have mercy, and I will have compassion on whom I will have compassion.*

However does the Holy God we serve let us keep our sins and fellowship with devils? Is self-pity evil?

1 Corinthians 10:20 *But I say, that the things which the Gentiles sacrifice, they sacrifice to devils, and not to God: and I would not that ye should have fellowship with devils.*

So then the believer will need to address self-pity in order to find freedom and break the curses in their life. Sometimes you hear about someone losing the healing. It's possible that they were never really healed, because if the devil can put diseases on you he can certainly relinquish them if it serves his purpose.

Our Mind and Health

King David played the anointed music and the spirit of insanity, and the tormenting spirits left King Saul for a little while, because those evil things can not stand listening to worship music. But soon after the worship music stopped being played, King Saul probably slipped back into self-pity and the tormenting spirits came flooding back onto him.

A poison like strychnine is rather invisible and can kill you as it is a colorless crystalline alkaloid used as a pesticide, particularly for killing rodents.

When Strychnine is ingested, it causes muscular convulsions and eventually brings death through asphyxia or sheer exhaustion.

Strychnine is one of the bitterest substances known. Its taste is detectable in very low concentrations. Still it can be hidden in some foods.

I like to say it this way, Self-pity is like the poison strychnine in that, it makes your life taste bitter until death eventually results.

The main gland of the limbic system, the hypothalamus, which we often call the brain of the endocrine system, will respond to your thought life. This is very important; it can only produce chemicals in response to what is going on deep within your soul and spirit. If you are entertaining a spirit of self–pity, that is going to be releasing those toxic chemicals like too much cortisol. At some point that means you are going to compromise your immune system, so the enemy of your soul is then able to bring sickness and diseases upon you. Now once you understand how this happens, you will be able to prevent it from continuing.

If someone breaks into your home, and burglarizes it, you are going to make sure that does not ever happen again, even if it means you acquire a trained attack watchdog.

We have been given the Holy Spirit who watches over us and does everything to help us make good choices. So we choose Godly pathways. Again this all has to start in our thought life, as much of our body's chemistry is directed by our thoughts.

Your body produces cortisol to suppress things like inflammatory response to the attack from allergies. An allergy is something that God did not design you with. Cortisol is actually a steroid hormone that is secreted by the adrenal cortex. An allergy is a hypersensitive reaction to any antigens, meaning any sort of substance that produces a reaction. When an antigen is introduced or entertained in your body, it stimulates the release and production of an antibody. This is any of the complex proteins produced by the B lymphocytes which are responding to the antigen.

It is more my personal observation here but I find so often when someone is suffering with a spirit of self-pity you will find they suffer from allergies. Coincident? I do not think so even though the person may appear to be such a saint at times. We are all a work in progress. However, again, we are dealing with our thought life here.

So be aware of what you think about. 2 Corinthians 10:5 *Casting down imaginations, and every high thing that exalteth itself against the knowledge of God, and bringing into captivity every thought to the obedience of Christ;*

Only you can control forest fires as well as your thought life.

The world is aware of self-pity, but in most cases they do not know how to effectively respond to it or deal with it on a spiritual level by applying the gospel. Often people end up being sent to secular professionals for help, who can only offer a pill to mask the problem which has dangerous side effects. I read a book called *Manufacturing Victims* written by a secular psychologist who exposed it as an industry that needs its patients to continue in therapy for as long as possible with a hefty fee attached each week. In the end hardly anyone is any better as they are wrongfully taught to co-exist with the evil spirits that they entertain. The Lord offers us a more excellent way.

Signs of Self-Pity

Self-pity is one of the most dangerous spirits coming from the enemy. It is extremely dangerous because it imprisons someone in self-centeredness. As a result, they cannot even think clearly enough or get a proper perspective on life. Being an artist, I had to learn to step back from my work in progress to get a proper perspective.

Besides, a spirit of fear that is behind self-pity gets you stuck without any real faith, no real hope, no real perspective on your life.

One of the best ways to break the power of self-pity is to simply stop comparing yourself to others by accepting that your life is what it is at the moment. Further, follow Christ's examples and commandments whilst you are waiting for Him to intervene.

Serve the Lord by helping others whilst you wait for your own problems to be resolved. The Lord says your reward will be your own healing.

Isaiah 58:6-8 *⁶Is not this the fast that I have chosen? to loose the bands of wickedness, to undo the heavy burdens, and to let the oppressed go free, and that ye break every yoke? ⁷Is it not to deal thy bread to the hungry, and that thou bring the poor that are cast out to thy house? when thou seest the naked, that thou cover him; and that thou hide not thyself from thine own flesh? ⁸Then shall thy light break forth as the morning, and thine health shall spring forth speedily: and thy righ-*

teousness shall go before thee; the glory of the LORD shall be thy reward.

As you seek Him and His righteousness first, all the things you need will be bestowed upon you.

I mean, you can pretty much overcome anything because all things are possible with God. And as we read in Romans 4:17, calling those things that are not as if they are. *(As it is written, I have made thee a father of many nations,) before him whom he believed, even God, who quickeneth the dead, and calleth those things which be not as though they were.* Romans 4:17

I've not seen one Scripture in all the Holy Bible that suggests we complain and grumble.

It did not work well for those in the Old Testament and it did not work well for those in the New Testament either.

In fact, while Paul and Silas were at Macedonia, they met with a lovely woman called Lydia.

Acts 16:13-15 *[13]And on the sabbath we went out of the city by a river side, where prayer was wont to be made; and we sat down, and spake unto the women which resorted thither. [14]And a certain woman named Lydia, a seller of purple, of the city of Thyatira, which worshipped God, heard us: whose heart the Lord opened, that she attended unto the things which were spoken of Paul. [15]And when she was baptized, and her household, she besought us, saying, If ye have judged me to be faithful to the Lord, come into my house, and abide there. And she constrained us.*

So while Paul was preaching the Gospel, Lydia who sold purple. She received the Word of God and was converted. Soon Lydia and her entire household were baptized. You know the Bible says to repent and be baptized to be saved. This was of course a complete emersion here.

Anyway Paul accepted her invitation and stayed at her house for a few days. Unexpectedly, in the next few days, a slave woman who had an evil spirit of fortune telling, showed up and started to follow Paul and Silas around, saying "These men are the servants of the most high God, which show unto us the way of salvation."

Here she was telling the truth—though you know the enemy will often give you a concoction of truth mixed with lies, she was indeed telling the truth and the Apostle Paul, being filled with the Holy Spirit at this time, felt rather put off and disturbed. He was grieved in His Spirit by what this fortune-telling-damsel-of-a-slave woman was saying to the people there (even though it was true). But Paul knew she needed to be saved and converted that she had tormenting evil spirits so he simply did something interesting here. Something the Lord Jesus taught him to do.

In Acts 16:18 *And this did she many days. But Paul, being grieved, turned and said to the spirit, I command thee in the name of Jesus Christ to come out of her. And he came out the same hour.*

It says he came out of her, being an evil spirit, which is a fallen angelic being that needs a body to manifest through to express its evil nature.

Now this is really interesting because this woman-slave-no-longer has the curse of fortune telling as the Holy Spirit embraced her in His love. Something must have really changed in her because soon her owners realized that she was not going to be making any more money with that cursed gift for them. Fortune telling of course is a counterfeit of the gift of knowledge and prophecy.

Acts 16:19-23 *[19]And when her masters saw that the hope of their gains was gone, they caught Paul and Silas, and drew them into the marketplace unto the rulers, [20]And brought them to the magistrates, saying, These men, being Jews, do exceedingly trouble our city,*

²¹And teach customs, which are not lawful for us to receive, neither to observe, being Romans. ²²And the multitude rose up together against them: and the magistrates rent off their clothes, and commanded to beat them. ²³And when they had laid many stripes upon them, they cast them into prison, charging the jailor to keep them safely:

So the people came against Paul and Silas and the magistrates gave the command that Paul and Silas should be beaten, chained, and thrown into jail. Do you see any evidence here of any spirit of self-pity with Paul and Silas? There is not even a hint, and they probably had bloody noses and many bruises but no self-pity. Those jails were most likely comparable to a sewer today—dark and smelly with rodents and biting insects.

As the story continues, at midnight Paul and Silas. with their backs wounded and bleeding, most likely must have been in a lot of pain from all their beatings, nonetheless, prayed, and sang praises unto God: whilst all the prisoners listened. I mean talk about putting on the sacrifice of praise here!

Then suddenly there was a great earthquake that the foundations of the prison shook. Immediately all the doors were opened, and the prisoner's heavy chains fell off them. At that moment, the keeper of the prison was awoken out of his sleep, and came running to the cells seeing the prison doors open, he drew out his sword, and would have killed himself, thinking by now all the prisoners had fled. But Paul cried with a loud voice, saying, "Do yourself no harm: for we are all here. Don't hurt yourself Mr. Jailer, everyone is still here."

You may be asking why he would kill himself. Well, in those days the punishment for letting the prisoners escape would have been worse than a short quick death, it would have been a torturous death.

I am not sure about you, but if I was beaten and bleeding and chained in prison, yet found the strength to put on the ultimate sacrifice of praise, and suddenly my chains fell off, the doors were open, and I had a chance to flee, I suspect I might have said, "Praise God the Lord has provided again," and I would be gone in a flash. But here Paul and Silas convinced themselves and the other prisoners to stay in jail. Paul must have been listening to the Holy Spirit because the prison guard knelt down before him and Silas and had a look of envy on his face. As a matter of fact, that very day, that prison guard and his entire household accepted the Lord Jesus Christ as their Savior, repented of their sins, and were baptized.

The prison guard had such a powerful conversion that he was even serving them proper meals, attending to their wounds and everyone was full of peace love and joy. No self-pity party here!

The next morning, the magistrate sent his servants to release Paul and Silas from prison. But Paul now refused to leave unless the magistrate himself came to tell them to go. That magistrate had a spirit of fear overtake him when he found out Paul was indeed a Roman citizen who had been wrongfully beaten, yet he came and begged Paul and Silas to go. They left the city once they were satisfied with the public release.

Morale of the story: I think you can overcome pretty much anything in this world when you stay in Faith and don't fall into complaining.

What would have happen if they said, "I don't believe this is happening to us, after all, look what we have done to share the Gospel?" A spirit of self-pity could have overcome them, and would have prevented the jailer and his family from being saved!

Self-pity is like dying a death that has no hope for a resurrection in it. It's like quicksand and even if the Lord Himself reached out from Heaven and offered to rescue you by His own hand, it won't happen because you have chosen to sink in despair.

We must understand that Self-pity is a spirit and helps support an unloving spirit. It comes from an evil kingdom of self. It is also full of a spirit of pride which consequently got Lucifer kicked out of heaven.

I find it interesting that most people suffering with self-pity are coincidently quite stubborn, pretty much mean spirited, and frankly don't understand why others act the way they do. It's because most people don't even know they have self-pity, but believe the people around them are their problem so the blame game begins. If a person has done all they know to find peace and joy, yet it evades them... more than likely this person is battling with self-pity.

Who is Entertaining You?

Self-pity has its own support group of spirits: Self-pity, on lead vocals, with ungodly grief and sorrow, singing back-up. Then victimization, the spirit of a broken heart, and hopelessness and despair play the instruments that come to try and kill, steal and destroy you.

This is not an all inclusive list, since self-pity works with many other spirits in concerts like matriarchal and patriarchal witchcraft, murmuring and complaining, accusation, spirits of depression all the unloving spirits which help support the major head liner—the spirit of fear.

All these spirits wreak havoc in our chemistry, and if left there, will cause us to respond unlovingly to any kind of offense. Because with a group of spirits like these, which are entertaining you, you have been programmed to respond negatively in a split second.

Actually this is very much like addictions: An addiction occurs when you are consumed with something and you cannot stop by an act of your free will. If the addiction has you then you have an addiction. Self-pity can certainly be an addiction.

A person with a spirit of self-pity will try to cause you to feel guilty to make you bend to their desires, which is manipulation and witchcraft.

Then you begin to have thoughts that something is wrong with you as those foul spirits work you over.

If you do not yield to the person with self-pity, they often explode in anger, or some sort of retaliation, which is the next way they try to control you. The person trying to control you also has a fear of loss of control and a spirit of control. So it's really matriarchal and patriarchal witchcraft working against you every time without exception.

Another way a spirit of self-pity manifests itself is to use disease and sickness to try and receive some love and attention from others. Which does not actually work because it only creates codependency doesn't it?

Then there is the false martyr attempt, which will draw attention to itself using self-pity. Because a true martyr will direct attention to God, as they decrease so the Lord can increase in them.

This world is headed into great tribulations; we have the Bible prophecies that tell us how it will play out. We have been warned by the Lord not to be ignorant of these times.

Luke 21:28 ²⁸*And when these things begin to come to pass, then look up, and lift up your heads; for your redemption draweth nigh.*

There are companies like Motorola which have invested millions in microchips which are as small as a grain of rice. They spent millions of dollars to discover that the best place to insert them is into the right hand or in the forehead. They have already produced billions of them. We are currently almost a cashless society. It would only take some sort of crisis to usher in a one world government that soon enforces that no one can buy or sell without the inserted microchip, or mark of the beast.

This is a time to get serious about the things of God.

If God spared Shadrach, Meshach, and Abednego from the fiery furnace as they stood in faith against a death sentence isn't that the same God we serve? The one who parted the Red Sea to save the Israelites can still do that for us today. No matter what tribulations we may have to face.

Romans 5:1-10 *¹Therefore being justified by faith, we have peace with God through our Lord Jesus Christ: ²By whom also we have access by faith into this grace wherein we stand, and rejoice in hope of the glory of God. ³And not only so, but we glory in tribulations also: knowing that tribulation worketh patience; ⁴And patience, experience; and experience, hope: ⁵And hope maketh not ashamed; because the love of God is shed abroad in our hearts by the Holy Ghost which is given unto us. ⁶For when we were yet without strength, in due time Christ died for the ungodly. ⁷For scarcely for a righteous man will one die: yet peradventure for a good man some would even dare to die. ⁸But God commendeth his love toward us, in that, while we were yet sinners, Christ died for us. ⁹Much more then, being now justified by his blood, we shall be saved from wrath through him. ¹⁰For if, when we were enemies, we were reconciled to God by the death of his Son, much more, being reconciled, we shall be saved by his life.*

How are we supposed to glory in tribulation? Unless you understand that you glory because tribulation is the first step to victory. If there were no trials and tribulations to go through, we would already be in Heaven.

We are called to be overcomers. Romans 12:21 *Be not overcome of evil, but overcome evil with good.*

John 16:33 *These things I have spoken unto you, that in me ye might have peace. In the world ye shall have tribulation: but be of good cheer; I have overcome the world.*

1 John 4:4 *Ye are of God, little children, and have overcome them: because greater is he that is in you, than he that is in the world.*

Revelation 3:21 *To him that overcometh will I grant to sit with me in my throne, even as I also overcame, and am set down with my Father in his throne.*

Revelation 12:11 A*nd they overcame him by the blood of the Lamb, and by the word of their testimony; and they loved not their lives unto the death.*

Revelation 17:14 *These shall make war with the Lamb, and the Lamb shall overcome them: for he is Lord of lords, and King of kings: and they that are with him are called, and chosen, and faithful.*

When you have overcome these things that you have overcome, they are no longer a problem.

This is part of the foundation of who you are in Christ as an overcomer, it is built in our new identity, in our DNA as a Child of God.

The things you overcome are the things you may not have to deal with very much again because you have perfected these things in your life by submitting them unto the Lord. You may still have to work on them at a deeper level here and there, but if you over come for example, feeling's of being rejected, then you are unlikely to participate with a spirit of rejection again because you recognize it upfront so it cannot take you captive again.

Practice Makes Perfect

The more I practiced my instrument the easier it was to play. We must practice being a doer of the Word.

James 1:22 *But be ye doers of the word, and not hear-*

ers only, deceiving your own selves.

Just as you might practice a piece of music until you can play it perfectly. You can't practice anything you want to accomplish unless you actually start practicing.

Unfortunately a spirit of Self-pity won't let you practice Holiness because it wants to keep you in bondage.

So it is really a process of sanctification... *knowing that tribulation worketh patience; and patience, experience; and experience, hope.* This is certainly a process, a pathway, a journey through this world, and through this is life.

Learning to ride a horse seemed easy and natural to me until I fell off one day. But I was taught as a child in equestrian school that if you ever fall off you need to get right back on if possible. When you fall off a horse you really feel like the wind has been knocked out of you and if you don't get up and get back on a spirit of fear is quite ready to work you over from then on. So you need to ride immediately to undo the trauma and replace it with a positive note.

We have all fallen down as Christians along the path here and there, fallen short of His glory, each one of us, and most of us got back up and kept on moving in His mercy, grace and love.

Unless, of course, you entertained a spirit of self-pity. Proverbs 24:16 *For a just man falleth seven times, and riseth up again: but the wicked shall fall into mischief.*

Start Overcoming Today

You will never start overcoming until you decide to start overcoming.

The people that our ministry has seen made free in Christ, were those who understood their spiritual battle and that self-pity was their enemy. They had to understand that there was still so much life to live after their self-pity party. Jesus came to give us a life more abundantly than we could ever imagine.

. So there is still a great plan for your life even after you may have experienced some failure, there is still a great plan for your life after you confess and over come some shameful sins. Why?... because God loves you.

In Christ we live and breath and belong. Self-pity wants to suffocate people so they cannot become overcomers.

What is the opposite of a spirit of self-pity? I believe it has to be a spirit of gratefulness. Just being thankful you are loved of God, being content with what you have, allows you to form a grateful heart.

That person who entertains a spirit of self-pity is not grateful for anything and not content. Being ungrateful invites the spirit of death to come slowly to take them out.

They entertain evil thoughts about how to kill themselves... Not realizing they will only wake up on the other side of death fully conscious and probably in a place for all eternity no one should ever desire to go to. It surely won't be "a heaven of a day" there, and once you are there, there is no escape.

All they have really done is simply change dimensions and will have the same horrible torment they had on this side.

It surely is better to face it here where you can still do something about it. I can tell you with great confidence and personal experience that there is life after death for everyone who was ever born.

Whether you have a body or not, does not keep you from existing as an eternal spirit being. People who have listened to the lies of the devil through Theta brain waves and ended up killing themselves, soon found out there was no benefit to it and it only made the situation much worse. Even though you are now on the other side without a body, you still have a soul and a spirit and your memories. So now you find you are in the same torment, only now you can't do anything more about it. How incredibly sad are those who trusted in the devil for answers and solutions.

Truthfully, a spirit of self-pity's tears just gets wet. They are like Crocodile's tears, an insincere display of emotion like a hypocrite crying fake tears of grief. Crocodiles tears are not authentic because crocodiles cannot cry like people do. They possess something called a lacrimal gland which secrete a proteinaceous fluid, just like in humans, which are visible after a crocodile is out of the water for a prolonged period of time, and the eyes begin to dry out.

I think Shakespeare got it right in Othello Act IV, Scene 1 "O devil, devil! If that the earth could teem with woman's tears, each drop she falls would prove a crocodile."

1 Thessalonians 5:18-23 *[18]In every thing give thanks: for this is the will of God in Christ Jesus concerning you. [19]Quench not the Spirit. [20]Despise not prophesyings. [21]Prove all things; hold fast that which is good. [22]Abstain from all appearance of evil. [23]And the very God of peace sanctify you wholly; and I pray God your whole spirit and soul and body be preserved blameless unto the coming of our Lord Jesus Christ.*

Practical Application

Do you have to put up with things that are going wrong in your life? Since they are going to happen from time to time, wouldn't it be easier to overcome them by having a good attitude?

When you are facing a problem, you still have to work it out. A spirit of fear will prevent you, but the Holy Spirit will guide you in all righteousness. Most problems just don't go away, you still have to work them out. As you are working out your salvation everyday, you might as well work out all your problems in faith with a good attitude. This will help you hear the Lord clearly if you are not all tied up in knots inside over some issue.

God does miraculous things when you stay in faith.

Psalm 46:1-2 *¹God is our refuge and strength, a very present help in trouble. ²Therefore will not we fear, though the earth be removed, and though the mountains be carried into the midst of the sea;*

Psalm 46:10 *Be still, and know that I [am] God: I will be exalted among the heathen, I will be exalted in the earth.*

We are just going to have to trust God!

Have you ever noticed that people with self-pity can never be pleased no matter how hard you try to please them? You cannot do enough for them and whatever you do is not enough to satisfy them, because they have this negative ungratefulness and unthankful heart that the devil has encased in some hard invisible wall. Always keep in mind that any evil spirit manifesting in a person can never be satisfied, because they have the person in torment.

How many songs have been written about unrequited love when truthfully they were probably only dealing with the spirit of self-pity in them?

When you try and love someone with self-pity they just push you away. The unloving spirit in them can not understand why you even want to be with them.

What does the Word of God say?

Romans 1:21-32 *²¹Because that, when they knew God, they glorified him not as God, neither were thankful; but became vain in their imaginations, and their foolish heart was darkened. [22]Professing themselves to be wise, they became fools, [23]And changed the glory of the uncorruptible God into an image made like to corruptible man, and to birds, and fourfooted beasts, and creeping things. [24]Wherefore God also gave them up to uncleanness through the lusts of their own hearts, to dishonour their own bodies between themselves: [25]Who changed the truth of God into a lie, and worshipped and served the creature more than the Creator, who is blessed for ever. Amen.*

[26]For this cause God gave them up unto vile affections: for even their women did change the natural use into that which is against nature: [27]And likewise also the men, leaving the natural use of the woman, burned in their lust one toward another; men with men working that which is unseemly, and receiving in themselves that recompence of their error which was meet. [28]And even as they did not like to retain God in their knowledge, God gave them over to a reprobate mind, to do those things which are not convenient; [29]Being filled with all unrighteousness, fornication, wickedness, covetousness, maliciousness; full of envy, murder, debate, deceit, malignity; whisperers, [30]Backbiters, haters of God, despiteful, proud, boasters, inventors of evil things, disobedient to parents, [31]Without understanding, covenantbreakers, without natural affection, implacable, unmerciful: [32]Who knowing the judgment of God, that they which commit such things are worthy of death, not only do the same, but have pleasure in them that do them.

Here is a perfect example of not taking every thought captive to the obedience of Christ. And today our world is suffering the consequence of not obeying God's commandments.

Self-pity is a powerful enemy and it has this nation and others in addiction to it. It is selfish and it is prideful and scriptures tell us that God will only exalt the humble who come before Him.

If you ever feel like you have lost your joy in the Lord, this is a good place to start again. The Joy of the Lord is the key, along with forgiveness for yourself and others that can open your heart to receive miracles.

We have examined some of the personalities of self-pity and personalities of fear. How sad it is to see that the devil has brought such evil upon people. How wonderful to know God can deliver you from all things including this.

Most of you know that a spirit of Rejection works closely with self-pity. Where there is strife, there is every evil thing. It works with hopelessness and despair, ungodly grief and sorrow, spirit of a broken heart and victimization. So you say things as if you're hypnotized and what you are saying. This all occurs because that foul spirit wants to cause as much wounding, and defilement as it can, through confusion and deceit.

That spirit of self-pity can make you feel quite numb to love, where you simply cannot feel love from God or others, even with yourself.

It is time to quit looking at your past, which cannot be changed now, and be here now to receive the Father's love in Christ Jesus.

Many of God's people are walking aimlessly with broken hearts and we wonder why the churches are not accomplishing very much today. Where are the great revivals?

How can you have great revivals without understanding there is more to being a Christian than just praying the prayer of salvation. That is a good place to start, but seems too many are clueless after that first step. Why is that? Because they aren't being taught how to follow Christ. We are told to make disciples of all men, so that they in turn can live according to the gospel truth and in turn, make disciples too. Many people are *destroyed* for lack of knowledge, and that's where many

Christians are today. Their lives aren't being blessed, it seems the destroyer is at the door. And one of those destroyers is self-pity.

So basically the spirit of self-pity is very occultic because it hides the truth. It's sorcery keeps you bound up so you keep going in circles and can't get free. Many churches keep telling you to renew your mind but how can you do that when unclean spirits are still ruling you, robbing you of the joy of the Lord?

Galatians 3:10 *Foolish Galatians, who hath bewitched you, that ye should not obey the truth, before whose eyes Jesus Christ hath been evidently set forth, crucified among you?*

How wonderful it is to be able to feel God's love and never doubt His Word to you and all the promises that come with it.

God loves you with an unconditional love. This has to be a deep-rooted revelation in your life. You cannot earn it, you must believe it and receive it, and be obedient to His Word.

John 14:15 *If ye love me, keep my commandments.*

Love is the Answer

You can actually love your family members unconditionally without expectations just as Christ loves you, but self-pity always requires something. There are conditions and expectations that will destroy you and your relationships, because self-pity has a void to fill, and wants to use you to get it, even if by bringing spirits of guilt and shame upon you to get you to love them somehow. Since these individuals have not been loved properly and have not been treated right, that spirit of self-pity wants to make you pay.

Faith, like Trust, comes from experience. We trust God by faith, but in most personal relationships we build trust from experience. That spirit of Self-pity will work to separate you from God, from yourself, and from others. You must beware, as this is one of the most vile evil spirits.

Let us always remember the Bible warns us to be careful of what we allow into our thought life.

Philippians 4:8 *Finally, brethren, whatsoever things are true, whatsoever things [are] honest, whatsoever things [are] just, whatsoever things [are] pure, whatsoever things [are] lovely, whatsoever things [are] of good report; if [there be] any virtue, and if [there be] any praise, think on these things. Those things, which ye have both learned, and received, and heard, and seen in me, do: and the God of peace shall be with you.*

A Proclamation

If you are really ready to get rid of this evil spirit that has been holding you down and disturbing your life such a long time. Speak aloud the following prayer so both invisible kingdoms will hear you

"Papa God, I renounce in my generations all the way back to Adam, on both sides of my family line, for fellowshipping with a spirit of Self-pity coming out of all accusing spirits, either accusing others or feeling accused by others and for feeling sorry for myself. I renounce and repent in my life for all condemnation and gossip and murmuring and discontentment and unthankfulness. For all Accusations towards You, myself and others. I repent for all Bitterness with all its underlings of Offense Rebellion, Programming, Control, Manipulation, Personality of Accusation, Prefabricated Personality, Comparing myself to others, Competition, Replay, Suspicion, Judging Others, Misunderstandings, Racism, Envy and Jealousy, feeling or being like a Scapegoat, Unworthy, Shame, Guilt, Isolation, Division, Self-pity, Fear, Lying, Perfectionism, Torment, the Destroyer, All Luciferian Spirits of Accusation. I thank You Papa God for Your forgive-

ness and I choose to receive it, I choose to walk
in freedom this day In Jesus of Nazareth name.
Amen"

As a minister of the gospel, this prayer is for you:

Lord, as your representative in the name of Jesus
Christ of Nazareth, I take authority over all the works of
the enemy and I bind and break its powers. I cancel the
assignment of every stinking spirit of self-pity and all
accusation. I bind all judgment and criticism, all condemnation, all gossip and murmuring. I bind and break
the powers of all accusation and criticism that would
come against you through the mouths of other people.
It is written, *"No weapon formed against you shall prosper and every tongue that rises against you in judgment
You shall condemn for this is the heritage of the servants
of the Lord! Their righteousness is of Me saith the Lord."*

I take authority over self-accusation where we accuse
ourselves, feeling we've not done enough, or not done
it well enough. I command every stinking evil spirit of
guilt, shame, condemnation, false burden bearing, false
responsibility, people pleasing, and driveness, discontentment and ungratefulness to go right now into the
dry place in the All Mighty and all powerful name of our
Lord Jesus Christ of Nazareth. I have been given authority to tread upon serpents and scorpions and over
all the powers of the enemy and nothing will by any
means harm us.

The Word of God is clear that as children of God, we
have been given the fruit of the Spirit which is love, joy,
and peace in the Holy Ghost. And this is what we are
willing to walk in from this day forward. Be released
now in the name of Jesus Christ of Nazareth. Amen"

Chapter 2

Minions of Self-pity

One of my heroes of the faith is General William Booth who founded the Salvation Army in England in the late 1800's. Booth must have believed as the early church did, as he too preached the Gospel, healed the sick and casted out devils. He also must have had the gift of prophecy because he wrote to someone and said this:

"In answer to your inquiry, I consider that the chief dangers which confront the coming century will be religion without the Holy Ghost, Christianity without Christ, forgiveness without repentance, salvation without regeneration, politics without God, and heaven without hell." (From a book called "Amazing Visions" - by David Ravenhill) All this has actually taken place now.

Doesn't that hit the nail on the head? I mean you can pretty much find all these false teachings out there now, and some are even gaining popularity.

In chapter one, we established that at the end of the day the spirit of self-pity is really protecting the spirit of Fear that God did not give you.

We know that Fear has torment. 1 John 4:18 *There is no fear in love; but perfect love casteth out fear: because fear hath torment. He that feareth is not made perfect in love.*

Someone suffering with self–pity will also be dealing with the spirit of fear. Again, self-pity is one of the most dangerous and vile spirits we have to deal with.

One thing we have seen in years of ministry is that the spirit of self-pity will also try to wear you out as a saint whilst you are trying to help make the captives free in Christ.

Because a spirit of self-pity appears to be the main

27

ingredient in all human pride, most of us have to fight that battle daily.

How many celebrities and world leaders have we heard boasting about their successes? This will remain a response to that spirit of pride manifesting itself unless they humble themselves and give the glory back to God as every believer should.

The voice of pride is really a spirit of boasting in the heart of someone who feels strong. Where as the voice of self-pity, also a form of pride, is the response of that spirit of pride causing suffering to someone who feels defeated and weak and ready to throw in the towel.

In 2 Corinthians Chapter 7 the Apostle Paul has some regrets for a moment that he wrote too strong a letter rebuking the Corinthian church. Getting confrontational is not something most of us look forward to doing. We might want to avoid it, or somehow rationalize it away, rather then actually confront it.

Paul, however, confronted the Corinthians directly, despite how much he stood to lose by doing so. The Corinthians had not just wronged him publicly but then they went ahead and even challenged his rightful authority as an Apostle. Paul was being attacked here and his reputation as Christ's ambassador was on the line. Yet his primary concern throughout this whole ordeal was to stay in right relationship to the Christ our Lord, and to bring the Gospel truth to the congregation in Corinth. Everything else he put aside, even the injustice and public humiliation that he must have suffered. And guess what?... there is not a hint of self-pity here.

2 Corinthians 7:1-4 *¹Having therefore these promises, dearly beloved, let us cleanse ourselves from all filthiness of the flesh and spirit, perfecting holiness in the fear of God. ²Receive us; we have wronged no man, we have corrupted no man, we have defrauded no man. ³I speak not this to condemn you: for I have said before, that ye are in our hearts to die and live with you. ⁴Great*

is my boldness of speech toward you, great is my glory-ing of you: I am filled with comfort, I am exceeding joyful in all our tribulation.

Paul continues saying in 2 Corinthians 7:14 *For if I have boasted any thing to him of you, I am not ashamed; but as we spake all things to you in truth, even so our boasting, which I made before Titus, is found a truth.*

It would have been easy for Paul to enter into self-pity here but instead he talks about how Godly sorrow works to bring you into repentance, which brings you into salvation and cleanses you from sin. All the rest is really just unrepentant sorrow and pain about something you lost, like a good friend, a good career, or loss of something that brought you pleasures. This can often be attributed to reaping what you have sown. If you plant corn, do not expect to grow tomatoes. If you want to know what your life will be like next year, listen to what you are saying now. Your words have great power and they will manifest what you continually speak. We will all reap what we have sown, even with our words.

Ecclesiastes 3:2 *A time to be born, and a time to die; a time to plant, and a time to pluck up that which is plant-ed;*

If you are suffering with a spirit of self-pity, it is really going to require some effort and some action on your part, it is not likely to just go away, or be rationalized away, as people try doing. How many times have you heard someone say, "But I am a good person compared to them?"

Never compare yourself to anyone else because you are a unique creation of the Lord.

Psalm 139:14 *I will praise thee; for I am fearfully and wonderfully made: marvellous are thy works; and that my soul knoweth right well.*

Pride and Self-Pity

You really need to be discerning here because a spirit of self-pity does not look like pride when you examine it on the surface because it appears to be so needy. But it is often a need that arrives from a wounded spirit of pride.

Self-pity will sound almost self-sacrificing like someone who says, "Oh Don't worry about me I will just sit here in the dark," when the power goes out.

Whereas people who tend to be boastful sound very self-sufficient, but again it comes from a spirit of pride. "I don't need any light I can find my way in the dark." Really?

This little light of mine I'm going to let it shine.

I have observed that a spirit of self-pity does not want to be seen as needy, but rather as a hero or heroine.

A spirit of self-pity will respond as a form of pride, putting on a display to others how much they are suffering. Again, this occurs because that spirit of self-pity is a form of self-idolatry.

1 Peter 5:4-11 *⁴And when the chief Shepherd shall appear,(which is our Lord Jesus, that great shepherd of the sheep, through the blood of the everlasting covenant, which we read in Hebrew 13:20) ye shall receive a crown of glory that fadeth not away.*

⁵Likewise, ye younger, submit yourselves unto the elder. Yea, all of you be subject one to another, and be clothed with humility: for God resisteth the proud, and giveth grace to the humble. (we as the church are to submit to one another as we stay humble before the Lord) ⁶Humble yourselves therefore under the mighty hand of God, that he may exalt you in due time: ⁷Casting all your care upon him; for he careth for you.

⁸Be sober, be vigilant; because your adversary the

devil, as a roaring lion, walketh about, seeking whom he may devour: ⁹Whom resist stedfast in the faith, knowing that the same afflictions are accomplished in your brethren that are in the world. (Again this referring to persecutions of a Christian in this world and not about diseases, as the word affliction here means the sufferings of Christ)

¹⁰But the God of all grace, who hath called us unto his eternal glory by Christ Jesus, after that ye have suffered a while, make you perfect, stablish, strengthen, settle you. (we suffer being persecuted for the Gospel sake) ¹¹To him be glory and dominion for ever and ever. Amen.

In other words, when a person agrees with a spirit of self-pity, which is also a form of boasting, then Papa God will resist you and the evil agreement he or she made with it.

I can look back retrospectively in my life and see those places where I did everything I could have possibly done to succeed or receive a healing and nothing seemed to happen. Why?

It was a result of that unfortunate agreement I had somehow made with the spirit of self-pity which was a form of pride that was hindering me from receiving the blessings of the Lord.

Isaiah 59:2 *But your iniquities have separated between you and your God, and your sins have hid his face from you, that he will not hear.*

I heard my friend, Pastor Henry Wright (Pleasant Valley Church, Thomaston GA) often state that he was not able to get one person healed or free that had self-pity. Because self-pity is the super glue that binds you to your past. Then the accuser is able to keep accusing you day and night whilst your stuck in it.

Self-pity basically looks *down* at your past, and those who refuse to listen to self-pity keep looking *up* to the glorious future that awaits every child of God.

Basically we could say that self-pity is *fear-based* and refusing to agree with self-pity is *faith-based*.

Again, every thought we have must travel a pathway of fear or faith! Which road will you take? Which thoughts will you entertain and dwell on? Which kingdom do you choose to live in?

Self-pity keeps you trapped in an invisible prison without any hope of escape or any hope of being freed.

1 Samuel 15:23-24 *²³For rebellion is as the sin of witchcraft, and stubbornness is as iniquity and idolatry. Because thou hast rejected the word of the LORD, he hath also rejected thee from being king. ²⁴And Saul said unto Samuel, I have sinned: for I have transgressed the commandment of the LORD, and thy words: because I feared the people, and obeyed their voice.*

Deceived by Self-Pity

King Saul fell into rebellion which the Bible says is witchcraft, and stubbornness, which is an iniquity— meaning a generational sin—is directly connected to the spirit of self-pity. Witchcraft is Occultism because stubbornness happens to be it's greatest contributor. Part of the spirits that support it is the spirit of being stubborn.

One major problem in dealing with the spirit of self-pity is that no one really wants to admit they are entertaining it. It's so very addictive and acts like a drug that keeps you numb to the real issues. It makes you so lethargic, you just want to sleep your life away. Truthfully it is probably the most addictive substance in the world.

As I stated before, most people suffering with self-pity are quite often stubborn, which makes them appear mean spirited, and it can be hard for a person to see that in themselves and to get rid of it.

Then they attempt to use the self-pity as a way to manipulate you to get any number of things. The classic example is people who are programmed to cry false tears to get their way and use the "poor pitiful me" to punish and control others.

I recall the sad story of one of the Pre-Raphaelite artists, Dante Gabriel Rossetti, who lived in the mid 1850's whose work I greatly admired growing up. He had this beautiful model named Lizzie Siddal and he fell in love with her, and instead of marrying her as he should have done which is still a bit of a mystery, he turned this innocent young woman into his mistress instead. Not cool.

She became totally dependent on him, after leaving her family and job thinking they would soon be married. One of the ways she eventually learned to try and control him was by not eating for several weeks at a time until he would break down and give her something she wanted.

In those Victorian times you can well imagine how difficult her situation had been as there was the possibility of marriage, yet now she had comprised herself by living with this Artist, who she found was not always faithful to her. During this relationship, Miss Siddell became a Christian, and I suspect that she may have withheld intimacy with Mr. Rossetti, as a form of control.

To deal with her situation, she ended up doing what people do today—she medicated herself not with the Word of God but with a drug. The drug of choice back then, which was readily available, was called Laudanum. It was a mixture of Opium and Alcohol. Many of the lower classes used it in England at that time. They even gave it to babies and young children to keep them quiet, not understanding they were actually turning them into addicts.

Sadly, when she was on her death bed, Mr. Rossetti

finally married her, giving her the one thing she had so desired. Unfortunately she had overdosed on the Laudanum and died. How wonderful that she had become a Christian, but sadly no one was there teaching her a more excellent way at that time. How many suffer today by not being properly discipled?

The strange thing about the spirit of self-pity is that it always has to blame someone, even if the person it blames is themselves, as poor Miss. Lizzie Siddall must have done.

Self-pity really is out to kill, steal and destroy you, and it is a self-perpetuating downward spiral to the depth of despair until it finds a way to completely take you out of action.

We learn early on to use self-pity

Children are often really helpless in many situations when they are young, unlike horses which can run with the herd for protection, hours after they are born.

In a way, children may use some sense of self-pity as a survival tactic, for example, you are in a store with them and they say, "if you don't give me candy I will hold my breath until I turn purple and then you'll be sorry," But when you see an adult in self-pity throwing a fit like a child, it really looks pitiful, as though they are sucking their thumb. In both instances, they have a real need for reassurance that someone loves them.

As we have seen already, self-pity is quite literally built on the spirit of fear, and it will often tell its victim, "no one is ever going to treat you right, or give you the proper respect you deserve."

So here are the ingredients that go into a pity-party:

- Self-pity

- Sprinkle in some anger and rage

- Add a few drops of jealousy and envy

- Throw in a handful of resentment and bitterness

- And before it is even fully baked it will start attacking someone

You will hear that spirit speak to you and tell you, "They never treated you right, and you are going to make them pay."

Fear vs. Faith

You must either be in faith or you are going to respond in fear.

Fear and faith are equal in this dimension, both in a sense demand to be fulfilled. Because both must project into the future. Without staying in faith, it is impossible to please the Lord, and that is a major problem.

Hebrews 11:1 *Now faith is the substance of things hoped for, the evidence of things not seen.*

So *faith* is an actual substance of things hoped for which bring on good things that God has for you, where as *fear* is an actual substance of things not hoped for— all the bad things you do not want to happen.

Hebrews 11:6 *But without faith [it is] impossible to please [him]: for he that cometh to God must believe that he is, and [that] he is a rewarder of them that diligently seek him. (that means you are seriously doing everything you can to obey the Lord because you believe Him at His Word and He sent His Word to bless you.)*

Psalm 107:20 *He sent his word, and healed them, and delivered them from their destructions.*

Now consider this: when you entertain a spirit of fear, what does it really do? If you answered it removes your faith, then you are correct. Because without faith it is impossible to please God. So when your faith is removed, who are you pleasing now?

Why do you think the devil is called the great deceiver? Because he really is great at deceiving people.

The devil has sneakily entered into people's lives early on by bringing in some emotional or verbal abuse, which can begin as early as childhood. Sometimes that even leads to physical and sexual abuse.

Or consider familiar spirits that gain access generationally, and so one ends up growing up in a legalistic and performance oriented family. So no matter what you did it was never quite good enough. How well did you meet the expectations of your parents? Did that unclean spirit make you feel like you were a disappointment to them?

Along with the spirit of trauma, rejection, abandonment and betrayal, the devil has brought in the spirit of self-pity to hold it all together, leaving feelings of discouragement and helplessness.

1 John 4:18 *"There is no fear in love, because fear has torment."*

If you're loved by people, you won't be afraid of them. If you experience God's awesome love, you will be filled with His holy joy and will be free to go about and accomplish what His purpose for your life is.

Anything else you depend on outside of God's holy joy will surely end up disappointing you at some point.

If your happiness depends on someone else, they will surely disappoint you along the way. If your happiness depends on some action or reaction by someone, you will be disappointed at some point as well.

The Antidote is Joy

Psalm 37:4 *Delight thyself also in the LORD; and he shall give thee the desires of thine heart.*

Matthew 25:21 *His lord said unto him, Well done, thou*

*good and faithful servant: thou hast been faithful over a
few things, I will make thee ruler over many things: enter
thou into the joy of thy lord.*

Nehemiah 8:10 *Then he said unto them, Go your way,
eat the fat, and drink the sweet, and send portions unto
them for whom nothing is prepared: for this day is holy
unto our LORD: neither be ye sorry; for the joy of the
LORD is your strength.*

Philippians 4:4 *Rejoice in the Lord always. Again I will
say, rejoice!*

If you lose your joy, you are an easy access to the enemy of your souls.

In other words, joy comes directly from the Lord when
you know Him and trust Him to take care of you and
every detail of your life.

Joy must start in your *thought life* from the inside to
outward expressions and it will gain strength and mo-
mentum from spending time in the Word.

I can recall quite a few celebrities I was friends with in
the world of music and film with whom had what most
people would think could bring you joy. They had fame
and fortune and could do whatever they pleased and
yet true joy was still not present.

True fulfillment and happiness will not be a result of
certain times and events or where you happen to live,
as those things are not lasting. The real joy everyone
is after was placed in you the moment you were saved
and converted and filled that empty space that was re-
served only for the Holy Ghost in you.

There should not be any room in your holy temples
except for you and the Holy Ghost. The problem begins
when you were back entertaining and fellowshipping
with devils, after the Lord forgave all your sins and
washed you clean from all unrighteousness.

God is very protective.

1 Corinthians 10:20 *But I say, that the things which the Gentiles sacrifice, they sacrifice to devils, and not to God: and I would not that ye should have fellowship with devils.*

Thankfully being God He knew we were going to fall short of His glory and struggle at times with being sinning saints. So He made provision for us like in 1 John 1:9-10 *If we confess our sins, he is faithful and just to forgive us our sins, and to cleanse us from all unrighteousness. If we say that we have not sinned, we make him a liar, and his word is not in us.*

Keeping a Heavenly Perspective

The spirit of self-pity can easily prey on someone who bases their joy and happiness on worldly things. It is vital that we understand this and keep a heavenly perspective or we shall find ourselves on an emotional roller coaster. Peter actually did walk a while on water as long as he kept his eyes on the Lord Jesus, but when he took his eyes off Jesus, He fell. We are going to have to do the same thing and walk in faith as the Word tells us:

Matthew 6:19-20 [19]*Lay not up for yourselves treasures upon earth, where moth and rust doth corrupt, and where thieves break through and steal:* [20]*But lay up for yourselves treasures in heaven, where neither moth nor rust doth corrupt, and where thieves do not break through nor steal.*

To lay up treasures in heaven means to be fully consecrated (dedicated) to God and to help all those who are in need. Even bringing someone a cup of cold water will be rewarded in Heaven as stated in Matthew 10:40-42.

Matthew 6:21 *For where your treasure is, there will your heart be also.*

This is why we are advised to keep in mind:

Colossians 3:1-4 *¹If ye then be risen with Christ, seek those things which are above, where Christ sitteth on the right hand of God. ²Set your affection on things above, not on things on the earth. ³For ye are dead, and your life is hid with Christ in God. ⁴When Christ, who is our life, shall appear, then shall ye also appear with him in glory.*

We are challenged to keep a Heavenly perspective as children of God. I learned as an Artist that I had to stand back from my work to get a proper perspective. We as Christians need to *stand back* at times and get "*the Big Picture*" here.

When we read what the Apostle John experienced in Revelation, just as it must have encouraged the weary persecuted saints of Asia Minor in that day, it still encourages us by giving us a heavenly perspective.

Those saints of old were experiencing many sufferings, and just hearing of John's experiences must have encouraged them as it helped them to rise above the details of their personal struggle to see "the big picture" that God had shown him.

The Word, Revelation, from the Greek word transliterates as 'apocalypse'—meaning the unveiling of something previously hidden.

In other words, Revelation here is like a window or television/video screen that allows you to see into the invisible, yet very real world, of Heaven.

It brings you encouragement right now to keep pressing on because you can see how awesome it will eventually be. Like finishing a degree in college, running a race or getting married, after a long engagement you keep pressing on towards the finish line.

You might be in the midst of a battle right now, but knowing where you will be spending eternity should help you be an overcomer as the Bible basically here is unveiling some of the mysterious parts of Heaven to comfort and bring us encouragement right now.

Eternal Words Outweigh the Present

Throughout the book of Revelation, the Apostle John describes the mysterious world that God revealed to him.

Receiving this Revelation of heaven certainly gave the Apostle John a fresh perspective on his own sufferings.

It appears rather obvious to me that Papa God had not given the Apostle John this supernatural experience just for his own benefit and personal knowledge. Rather, this is a message from the throne-room of Heaven, for all the persecuted and weary saints of God, to stay focused and keep pressing on, stay the course, remain encouraged, and keep on keeping on.

When difficult things happen to you, the enemy of our souls is right there to try and help you feel all the emotions and pain that accompany of trials you are facing, by releasing all those memes molecules.

Then a chain reaction begins. Your hypothalamus is stimulated (which acts like the brain of your endocrine system) by building a memory. So for example, if you lost someone you loved dearly in some sort of fatal accident, then the next funeral you attend, (hopefully not too soon after) will tap into that memory and replay all the feelings and pictures associated with the previous funeral which intensifies the present situation.

The enemy understands that your hypothalamus is the real heart of endocrine or hormonal system, which responds to your thought life, and will therefore attack it relentlessly.

This is the gland that releases the chemicals related to your emotions, which is attached to the thought. So in other words the enemy gives you a thought and that causes your body to react to it. Then the spirit of fear, which God did not give you, begins to take control to get you to submit to its request, which will bring you some degree of torment.

1 John 4:18 *There is no fear in love; but perfect love casteth out fear: because fear hath torment. He that feareth is not made perfect in love.*

If you agree with the spirit of fear and allow it into your thoughts, then it will train you in sinful ways and cause the release of toxic chemicals that begin to breakdown your body and break down your life.

The enemy knows that if he can bring you to a certain place in your thought life, which is where he has been training you for probably many years in unrighteous thinking or what the Bible calls building up "strong holds," you will have a tendency to somewhat exaggerate your troubles, presenting them as being even worse than they actually are.

The enemy will cause you to lose your focus, distracting your eyes from the Lord, and will take you out of faith and bring you into fear or torment which are basically interchangeable at this level. An illness like high blood pressure are really the result of the enemy training you over the years to have fear of tomorrow, causing you to not trust the Lord for all things.

When the Lord opened the Apostle John's spiritual eyes and permitted him to see inside Heaven, and describe in some details for the rest of us, that eternal dimension. It must have been to encourage those who have grown weary in well-doing as Christians. Let's face it, in this world there are daily conflicts, and the spirit of self-pity is all about keeping you wrapped up in self, rather then serving the Kingdom. Self-pity is all about the kingdom of self!

The Bible from Genesis to Revelation essentially lets

us get a glimpse to see through a window into Heaven. John's revelation surely encouraged those weary first century believers the way it still encourages us today. There are five major themes that truly emerge in the book of Revelations that harmonize with the entire Bible: (1) The Glory of Christ; (2) The Sovereignty of Christ; (3) The Worship of Heaven; (4) Spiritual Warfare; (5) The Second Coming of Christ.

When you step back and get a proper perspective on this, you begin to see the big picture.

We believers all need some encouragement from time to time in this world. We try to stay faithful to the Lord in a world that is really rather antagonistic to Christians.

John, being imprisoned when the Holy Spirit caused him to write this vision down, was surely suffering being persecuted for Christ's sake.

Behind the Curtain

The Holy Spirit came to offer this encouragement to John by drawing the curtains of Heaven back a bit and permitting him to see into the invisible world of spiritual realities—thus showing him a preview of what will happen when he finally arrives.

Read the account of what John saw for yourself, it may help give you a proper heavenly perspective even now.

It surely must have had the same effect of giving the early Christians a proper perspective by enlarging the vision of those early believers who were living in hostile enemy territory. Knowing how the story ends gave them the incentive to keep going, as it should for us today.

The Spirit of God encourages us to endure and persevere as good and faithful soldiers of Jesus Christ of Nazareth. We simply must follow orders and do what we are supposed to do. This way they will know we are

Christians by our love.

When you realize there are multitudes of angels, angelic beings and people who have graduated from earth, up there right now in heaven all singing some triumphant chorus of praise to the Lamb of God, which will be a totally amazing musical experience, you shall be encouraged to continue to praise Him here on earth.

By giving us a preview of some of the coming attractions, like the Second Coming of the Lord Jesus Christ of Nazareth as our Mighty Conqueror, we are motivated to be faithful unto death as the early first century believers were.

Studying the Book of Revelation helps us destroy the spirits of doubt and unbelief that try and attack all believers. How can you entertain a spirit of self-pity when you think on such things? How can you stay discouraged when you are reminded that the resurrected Lord Jesus is really doing all He can to help orchestrate things to bless us. No matter how difficult a situation may be at the moment. We still need to walk in faith, not based on how it may look right now. We need to be reminded that He will take care of us and remind us that He is coming for us.

Our battle cry needs to be "hold the fort brothers and sisters, Christ is coming for us."

Remembering History

Since coming here to Atlanta, I learned that the civil war is still being talked about. I learned that there was a Northern General named Sherman that came with the Union army and really besieged Atlanta.

There was also this Confederate fellow named General Hood, who took a noble stand against Sherman's troops at Alatoona Pass.

As General Sherman was watching the battle from a safe place on Kennesaw Mountain, it became clear that General Hood's army had began to prevail in the battle. To rally his troops, Sherman needed to rally his men not to give up and so he used a system called *heliographed*. This was a device for communicating over some distances using light from the sun reflected in mirrors to flash signals in Morse code or some other sort of secret code messaging system. Apparently his message read, "Hold the fort, for I am coming." As that message was passed from soldier to soldier, the army gained courage and won a victory.

It appears that was really the motivation for a believer named Phillip Bliss' to write a popular hymn in his day:

"Hold the fort, for I am coming, Jesus signals still; Wave the answer back to heaven, By thy grace, we will."

Our Commander and Chief, the Lord Jesus, tells us in Revelation 22:12 *And, behold, I come quickly; and my reward is with me, to give every man according as his work shall be.*

Will we take courage in this? By His grace we will.

James 1:8 *A double minded man [is] unstable in all his ways.*

Being double-minded is like you are trying to fight for both armies, you are going back and forth and don't know what side of the battle you are on. You can get badly hurt that way, and even be labeled as a traitor.

When you entertain a spirit of Fear you are being double-minded and what does it really do? It removes your faith. If without faith it is impossible to please God then when you enter into an agreement with the spirit of fear and your faith is removed, who are you really pleasing?

Practical Application

Let us do all we can to stay in faith, stay in the Word and trust that the Lord will do those things that seem impossible. Continue in praise and worship with a thankful heart, no matter what is going on in your life. Continue thanking Him for what He has already done. Remember, a thankful heart is a heart that receives.

Philippians 4:19 *But my God shall supply all your need according to his riches in glory by Christ Jesus.*

Pray this prayer if you are ready to get rid of this evil spirit that has been holding you down and disturbing your life for such a long time:

Papa God, here I am again recognizing even more places that I have allowed the enemy in my life. I need Your forgiveness and I come now to forgive all those who have sinned against me, including myself.

I want and need You Lord to wash me clean again from all filthy things of the flesh and spirit that have set up strong holds in my thinking processes. I trust You Lord that You are working on perfecting holiness in me and I love You Lord and I thank You Lord.

That as many times as I need to ask Your forgiveness I am so very grateful to know that You are so quick to forgive me and wash me clean again and help me stay on this narrow path that leads to your Gates of Heaven. I am so grateful that You have prepared a place for me there and I will be with you forever in eternity, in the New Heavens and New Earth to see the New Jerusalem.

Lord I want to be faithful and obey Your every commandment.

I want to pray now and renounce in my generations all the way back to Adam and repent in my life for fellowshipping with any unclean evil spirits I have recognized this day.

For all the old selfish programming I allowed in

with the spirit of self-pity. For all the places even this past week that I felt like someone was accusing me or that I may have accused someone else somehow. I ask that I be forgiven now as I forgive them also, so that I can accept your most gracious forgiveness and even forgive myself through the precious blood of Jesus Christ of Nazareth.

Having forgiven them now Lord, I confess any sin on my part towards them or anyone else.

(Take a moment and speak alone to the Lord here confess those things)

Now Lord I declare that You and You alone are my God and my King the one in whom I trust and place my allegiance, and besides You there is no other and I am here to praise You and Worship You Lord. To submit myself to You in unreserved obedience.

I now recognize that the devil has sent evil spirits that want to make me feel sorry for myself. But I refuse to listen to the enemy lying to me.

I only want to hear You my Lord that only Your voice will I obey and follow. And having submitted to You now as Your Holy Word directs me to do, I am able to resist the devil and his fallen evil kingdom. I am able to resist the temptations, and all the pressure of his attacks on my life. I am able to see through the devils; lies and deceptions and anyone he tries to use as his instrument to manifest evil through. I shall resist the devil everyway possible and make him flee from me. I drive him away from me and my family and business and exclude him from interfering in the all powerful name of Jesus Christ of Nazareth.

So right now I specifically reject and cast out of myself every unclean spirit of infirmity and infection, all inflammation, all malignancies, all allergies, all pain and spirits of pain. All viruses and sickness and every form of rebellion and witchcraft.

I thank You again Papa God that through the precious spilt blood sacrifice of Your only begotten Son Jesus Christ of Nazareth on that cross that as a spirit-filled born again believer I have passed out from under the curse, and have entered into the blessings of Abraham, who You blessed in All things. Lord I am ready and want to walk in blessings and Your favour that I am able to walk in divine health and prosper in all good things.

I give You all the praise and honour and glory. Amen

Now I want to pray for you:

Lord as Your representative in the name of Jesus Christ of Nazareth, I take authority over all the works of the enemy and I cast out every unclean spirit of infirmity and infection, all inflammation, all malignancies, all allergies, all pain and spirits of pain. All viruses and sickness and every form of rebellion and witchcraft that every unclean evil spirit named now has to come up and out and leave this child of God, and not enter into them again. You must go right now into the dry place in the all mighty and all powerful name of my Lord Jesus Christ of Nazareth. I have been given authority to tread upon serpents and scorpions and over all the powers of the enemy and nothing will by any means harm us. If I by the finger of God can cast out devils, know that the Kingdom of God has come unto you.

Now may each of you be overwhelmed in the love and the Joy of the Lord.

Be released now in the name of Jesus Christ of Nazareth. Amen

Chapter 3

The Mind of the Spirit of Self-Pity

As we have been exposing the spirit of self-pity in the last two chapters, I also want to show you about how the Lord gives us the same kind of encouragement He gave the Apostle John to see into the next world to tell us enough to keep us pressing in and keep marching on, keep fighting the good fight of faith.

If we all rode horses this world would be much more stabilized. I recall Sir. Winston Churchill had once said –'There is something about the outside of a horse that is good for the inside of a man." ~

I would agree with that statement because as an equestrian, I have personally experienced this over many years. Sir Winston also said—"No hour of life is wasted that is spent in the saddle."

I think one reason dogs and horses always seem happy is that they are not really trying to impress anyone. My dog and horse know they are part of our family and they certainly got that agape love thing down rather well.

Come to think about it, most dogs I have known seem kinder and more caring then many people I have known.

Still it is always curious to me that I have observed, especially in horses, how they can be so brave and strong and magnificent in one moment, and in the next become like cowards and run. The Lord designed them with that fight-or-flight reflex, so they almost seem double-minded at times because they move fast instinctually. It takes a lot of training to convince them not to bolt on you when they sense any danger.

Animals, for the most part, seem to read us like a

book and it's rather amazing to me how they know such things about us. It appears to me that their spirit is able to communicate with our spirit, otherwise, how would they know when we "feel" fear ourselves? Or if we don't like them?

There is an old saying, "It's a lot like nuts and bolts - if the rider's nuts, the horse bolts!

There is a horse whisperer named Pat Parelli, I had the pleasure to study with him a bit and paint a portrait of him and his horse some time ago. I recall he would come up with these really profound statements like the time he said, "A horse doesn't care how much you know, until he knows how much you care."

Mr. Parelli has an extraordinary way with horses and even with dogs.

I actually think that applies to people as well. Once someone understands how much you really care about them, it often builds a level of trust, or faith in the relationship. You then realize you can depend on them as a friend. How much more should we understand how much the Lord cares for us then?

1 Peter 5:7 *Casting all your care upon him; for he careth for you.*

Because we do not properly understand this, so many times we have to deal with a measure of double- mindedness—depending on where we are in our present understanding and knowledge of the Word of God.

When someone falls into the trap of being double-minded, they will easily be overcome with the spirit of self-pity, as soon as something does not go their way in which they wanted it.

They also begin having a problem because they have no real understanding of the love of God. There is a big difference between *knowing* God and *knowing about* God.

I happen to know about His royal Highness the Prince of Wales. Back when my wife and I lived in England, I was once invited to Buckingham Palace to personally deliver a watercolor painting I did for him. I knew several people that knew him and played polo with him on his team. But I personally can not say I really know the man I only know about him. I can however say I really know the Prince of Peace personally which certainly has much more eternal rewards and consequences.

Matthew 7:24-27 *24Therefore whosoever heareth these sayings of mine, and doeth them, I will liken him unto a wise man, which built his house upon a rock: 25And the rain descended, and the floods came, and the winds blew, and beat upon that house; and it fell not: for it was founded upon a rock. 26And every one that heareth these sayings of mine, and doeth them not, shall be likened unto a foolish man, which built his house upon the sand: 27And the rain descended, and the floods came, and the winds blew, and beat upon that house; and it fell: and great was the fall of it.*

Helping Others

When someone comes to you for help and comfort. and you recognize they have an unclean spirit of self-pity, you must be very careful to speak only as the Holy Spirit gives you words, because they will try to get you to become codependent with them in their self-pity, in their victimization and in their hopelessness and despair.

When they realize that you see through them, you must stay on guard because those evil spirits manifesting in them are going to start attacking you as soon as they realize you are not playing their game. You have to decide right then and there if you are going to be a man or woman of God and not enable them in their sins.

What happens is that they will often turn on you 180 degrees and then you will quickly become the object of their anger and rage. You must not accept that rubbish into your spirit, and you won't if you are able to recognize and discern what is really going on.

When they don't get their way even with really small things, they will fall off of the foundation they have built their house upon, which is really shifting sand, and they will go right back into their agreement with the spirit of self-pity.

As I have said before, being doubleminded really means that a person is partially walking in the kingdom of God and partially in the kingdom of Satan. It's like they are in that civil war story we shared earlier, they are fighting with the Northern Army and the Southern army at the same time. That is like being a double-agent and a traitor, and usually brings a very stern death sentence. The Bible tells us in:

Romans 6:23 *For the wages of sin is death; but the gift of God is eternal life through Jesus Christ our Lord.*

Again, we are all a work in progress, but we should see some progress and some good fruit along the journey.

Sometimes people are just dressing up for God, trying to look their best, trying to do things to get God's favor. But you should always keep in mind that Papa God is more concerned about how you look on the inside.

Matthew 7:15-20 *[15]Beware of false prophets, which come to you in sheep's clothing, but inwardly they are ravening wolves. [16]Ye shall know them by their fruits. Do men gather grapes of thorns, or figs of thistles? [17]Even so every good tree bringeth forth good fruit; but a corrupt tree bringeth forth evil fruit. [18]A good tree cannot bring forth evil fruit, neither can a corrupt tree bring forth good fruit. [19]Every tree that bringeth not forth good fruit is hewn down, and cast into the fire. [20]Wherefore by their fruits ye shall know them.*

As you are building your relationship with the Lord,

you will be drawn to spend time in His Word, which brings you into a place of prayer, and into praise, and worship and thanksgiving. Staying humble before Him with a grateful heart, is certainly the opposite of someone entertaining the spirit of self-pity.

John 14:26 *But the Comforter, which is the Holy Ghost, whom the Father will send in my name, he shall teach you all things, and bring all things to your remembrance, whatsoever I have said unto you.*

When someone falls deeply in love, their focus seems to be centered on the person with whom they are in love. They just want to be with that person all the time. Then we have all these songs and stories written about unrequited love situations.

Someone suffering with a spirit of self-pity is not able to be in a proper relationship of love. When you take two people together they become like one. If one of them becomes centered on self, they go back to being separated because it is then "all about me" instead of "all about us."

Isn't that what the Lord is telling us throughout the Bible? He has done everything possible to bring us into a place where we belong, making a way possible for us to be together forever through Jesus Christ of Nazareth.

The Lord our God has many positive and many negative statements that He has told His church.

Because of His great love and affection towards us it seems to me that He always focuses on the positive things first in order to prepare our hearts to receive whatever is needed for correction. When you understand someone loves you, you are more likely to be able to receive any correction. When you begin by telling someone the good things you see in them first, you are able to go after exposing the negative things.

By doing this, as the Lord does, we can possibly help

and encourage them to eliminate those evil and toxic things from their lives, tearing down the devils strongholds and building up and replacing the devils lies with God's Holy truth and righteousness.

Seven Churches

The Lord has some serious issues with seven churches mentioned in Revelation. Only the church of Philadelphia is really praised, but the rest He gives a stern correction.

Revelation 2:4 *Nevertheless I have somewhat against thee, because thou hast left thy first love.*

Amazingly, because of His love for His people, the Lord Jesus gives us three basic steps to take to recover ourselves for those who have ears to hear:

1. He tells the church to go ahead and remember your former condition, go ahead and recall what you were like before you were saved and converted.

   Stop right now and recall how you were when you first experienced Christ's love in the past, realize your current position and compare it to how you used to be.

2. Then the Lord tells us to Repent, stop sinning and change your direction, stop doing these negative, harmful things. Get your thoughts working for you instead of against you.

3. Go back and do the things you did at first, those things the Lord has called you to do, those positive things that bring blessings. Repentance is not just turning away from wrong things, it is also doing what is right in the sight of God.

How is it that only one church stayed true out of the seven groupings of Papa God's elect children? How were they able to understand the Lord Jesus' commission to carry on preaching the Gospel, healing the sick, and casting out demons? John 14:12 says greater things shall you do than Jesus even did!

This means anyone from every race and generation that comes to Christ, who is eager and keen and passionate about the things of God, who obey His commandments; such a believer will flow unlimited power to do the works of Christ.

Even though the other churches were given some awesome gifts and blessings from God, how come only the church of Philadelphia stayed true and did not become some sort of Christian social club with a grace on steroids message? Even though they saw some good things and had riches and popularity in the end, who wants to find out you took a lesser path and got lukewarm in your "faith and calling" so the Lord Jesus ends up vomiting you out of His mouth? After the Lord says some positive things He really gives a stern warning here.

Revelation 3:13 -17 *¹³He that hath an ear, let him hear what the Spirit saith unto the churches. ¹⁴And unto the angel of the church of the Laodiceans write; These things saith the Amen, the faithful and true witness, the beginning of the creation of God; ¹⁵I know thy works, that thou art neither cold nor hot: I would thou wert cold or hot.¹⁶So then because thou art lukewarm, and neither cold nor hot, I will spue thee out of my mouth. ¹⁷Because thou sayest, I am rich, and increased with goods, and have need of nothing; and knowest not that thou art wretched, and miserable, and poor, and blind, and naked:*

What is to become of the churches who only teach about salvation and not about sanctification?; who deny God still does healing and miracles when you line up in obedience with His Word?

Before the Lord gave this stern warning, He spoke about the positive things going on with the Church of Philadelphia as an example of what the church is supposed to look like. They were empowered with those supernatural gifts we read about in 1 Corinthians 12:4-11, and again in Romans 12:6-8, in order to reach out to the whole world with the total Gospel message, so that signs and wonders and miracles and healing are following you as you follow after the Lord Jesus Christ of Nazareth. That would be Biblical evangelism,

Revelation 3:6-12 *⁶He that hath an ear, let him hear what the Spirit saith unto the churches. ⁷And to the angel of the church in Philadelphia write; These things saith he that is holy, he that is true, he that hath the key of David, he that openeth, and no man shutteth; and shutteth, and no man openeth; ⁸I know thy works: behold, I have set before thee an open door, and no man can shut it: for thou hast a little strength, and hast kept my word, and hast not denied my name.*

⁹Behold, I will make them of the synagogue of Satan, which say they are Jews, and are not, but do lie; behold, I will make them to come and worship before thy feet, and to know that I have loved thee. ¹⁰Because thou hast kept the word of my patience, I also will keep thee from the hour of temptation, which shall come upon all the world, to try them that dwell upon the earth. ¹¹Behold, I come quickly: hold that fast which thou hast, that no man take thy crown. ¹²Him that overcometh will I make a pillar in the temple of my God, and he shall go no more out: and I will write upon him the name of my God, and the name of the city of my God, which is new Jerusalem, which cometh down out of heaven from my God: and I will write upon him my new name.

As you overcome and allow the Lord your God an all access pass to your holy temple, your body, your life, then the Lord will do an amazing work of washing you clean from all unrighteousness and filth of the flesh and spirit with the washing of the water of His Holy Word.

As you grow and mature in Christ's love, the fruits of the spirit will begin to appear in you and in your life as the laws of sowing and reaping play out.

If you plant good seeds and water and fertilize them good things will grow and good things will be harvested.

John 7:37-38 *³⁷In the last day, that great day of the feast, Jesus stood and cried, saying, If any man thirst, let him come unto me, and drink. ³⁸He that believeth on me, as the scripture hath said, out of his belly shall flow rivers of living water.*

Unfortunately, after some become believers, those who are not discipled properly, seem to fall into *trying* to do something for God, so they get into works. When you think it through, it is really just a form of religion, also known as religious spirits and legalism. The fact is, God does not need you to accomplish something for Him, until He can accomplish something in you.

Just as with your first love, your first real work is to really get to know Papa God, and build a relationship to let Him complete the work in you. Then you will manifest the fruits of the Holy Spirit, and the works of God, that He has assigned for you, will then be done through you. The Bible tells us.

Proverbs 21:2 *Every way of a man is right in his own eyes: but the LORD pondereth the hearts.*

Jeremiah 17:9-10 *⁹The heart is deceitful above all things, and desperately wicked: who can know it? ¹⁰I the LORD search the heart, I try the reins, even to give every man according to his ways, and according to the fruit of his doings.*

Psalm 139:23-24 *²³Search me, O God, and know my heart: try me, and know my thoughts: ²⁴And see if there be any wicked way in me, and lead me in the way everlasting.*

So the secrets of our hearts—all those secret motives and attitudes and perceptions—can only be truly revealed through relationship with the Lord Jesus.

The spirit of self-pity wants to separate you from your relationship with Jesus, with others and yourself, and won't let you be really loved, as the unloving spirit helps hold it in place.

All real relationships have to be constructed and built on faith and trust or you have some sort of deception going on.

We all go through some difficult things and situations in this fallen world. With words and actions sometime we end up being hurt or hurting others even when it was not in our hearts as a believer to do so. We are to always love one another as the Lord loves us. But when that does not happen, someone can be hurt and wounded.

As we practice our faith as Christians, we ought to be quick to respond in forgiveness, going straightway to the Lord and forgiving the offense or offender including yourself. We know that one major block to healing is unforgiveness. You certainly don't want to receive it as sin into your life, because without forgiving, you cannot be forgiven.

Who can afford to stay in un-forgiveness? Who wants to be in constant torment because you refuse to forgive everyone, including yourself?

In Matthew 18, the Lord Jesus taught a parable of a servant who was forgiven millions he owed the King and then went out after being forgiven and refused to forgive someone who owed him about the equivalent of $17.00.

When the King heard about how this man didn't show mercy and compassion for another who owed him money, he sent him to prison to be tortured until he paid back all the millions he owed the King in the first place. Which is certainly a word picture for us to understand how vital forgiveness and mercy is towards one another.

Matthew 18:34-35 [34]And his lord was wroth, and

delivered him to the tormentors, till he should pay all that was due unto him. ³⁵So likewise shall my heavenly Father do also unto you, if ye from your hearts forgive not every one his brother their trespasses.

We have to forgive everyone from our hearts whether we feel like it or not, recognize what is really going on in the spiritual places, bind those things and refuse them into our lives in the all mighty name of Jesus Christ of Nazareth.

If you offend someone or they offend you, go work it out with them as soon as possible. If they won't listen take two or three people with you, don't go telling loads of people trying to justify how you were in the right. God knows if you were in the right and He will deal with the situation as you obey His ways. When you go back to them, who are offended, and try and make your peace and they still refuse you, only then shall you tell the church and then pray for them, for they are like a heathen unbeliever not understanding the Gospel. Pray they get really saved and converted, and bless them by returning kindness for evil.

Matthew 5:44 *But I say unto you, Love your enemies, bless them that curse you, do good to them that hate you, and pray for them which despitefully use you, and persecute you;*

When someone is really wounded, it seems harder to help them recover and be healed, because after all, wounding is often deeper then just being a bit pierced here and there. It really comes down to a spirit of pride and idolatry, rebellion and stubbornness.

This is especially true when a person is refusing to even try to reconcile the relationship with you, before God, for whatever offence took place.

Sadly, some people will simply go down rather quickly, drowning in a spirit of self-pity after they've failed to work out some reconciliation. After not being able to sort things out the way they had hope for, then the enemy gets right in there with them causing them to start playing the blame game all together.

In the end both sides seem to be defiling each other as the spirit of self-pity overtakes them. It is very hard to keep trusting someone who lets you down and defiles you. All the more reason we need to maintain a grateful heart, and be thankful for what we do have.

A Personal Revelation

I recall a time when I was feeling really down, struggling with a misunderstanding between my management company and the record label. That spirit of self-pity was trying to overtake me simply because I was upset with the way my music was getting produced, as it was not heading in the direction I wanted it. It was the 80's and I was pretty much this hard rocker musician, as hard as that might be to realize. MTV just started, and my producers were pushing me into a musical form I was not comfortable with. So I was riding on a train in the underground, reading this book that had a quote in it about, "how I cried because I had no shoes until I saw a man who had no feet." As I read those lines, I happened to look up just in time to see a person without any arms or legs being pushed in a wheelchair.

As a young child, that was a life changing moment for me. I recall thinking, "Why am I so upset about this record I am doing, I have so many blessings." That moment changed my entire perception and outlook, and I haven't looked back since. Our Lord is so wonderful to us; no matter where we are on this journey, He is patient and willing to lead us into all truth and righteousness.

It is very humbling to say I had been wrong and had been entertaining an evil spirit of self-pity. But when we finally confess this, it is the first step towards obtaining freedom in the Lord.

1 John 1:9 *If we confess our sins, he is faithful and just to forgive us our sins, and to cleanse us from all unrighteousness.*

It's not like you can hide anything from God anyway.

Psalm 139:8 *If I ascend up into heaven, thou [art] there: if I make my bed in hell, behold, thou [art there].*

In a way, when you entertain a spirit of self-pity, you have actually brought some hell on earth instead of what you are supposed to bring—Heaven.

Matthew 6:9-10 *⁹After this manner therefore pray ye: Our Father which art in heaven, Hallowed be thy name. ¹⁰Thy kingdom come, Thy will be done in earth, as it is in heaven.*

If we are supposed to be having God's will be done on earth as it is in Heaven, and allow self-pity instead, we are not doing thy will in earth as it is in Heaven.

The highway to hell is going to be terrible all the way there, and hell itself will be much worse then anyone can image. It was made for the devil and not for you. There will be no escape, and demons will be tormenting people by doing unspeakable, horrible things that make the holocaust seem like a tea party. It will smell like sulfur all the time forever, and people will have their memories of life here on earth burning in a sea of fire, being tormented all the while.

The spirit of self-pity is bringing some hell on earth and there really seems to be no way out unless you are finally able to humble yourself before the Lord, thus allowing the Holy Spirit to lead you into discernment and knowledge.

John 8:32 *And ye shall know the truth, and the truth shall make you free.*

Hebrews 5:14 *But strong meat belongeth to them that are of full age, [even] those who by reason of use have their senses exercised to discern both good and evil.*

Basically when you come right down to it, that spirit of self-pity is separating you from Papa God, yourself, and others.

Because self-pity is a form of pride, you have exalted yourself against something that is greater than you and God. Whenever you bow down to something evil like the spirit of self-pity or a spirit of fear, God being a gentleman, will stand back and allow you to have your freedom of choice.

As you choose the devil's lies over God's Holy truth, you shouldn't wonder why your prayers are not being answered. Without faith it is impossible to please the Lord, and your sins cause God not to listen to you.

Isaiah 59:1-2 *¹Behold, the LORD's hand is not shortened, that it cannot save; neither his ear heavy, that it cannot hear: ²But your iniquities have separated between you and your God, and your sins have hid his face from you, that he will not hear.*

Jeremiah 5:25 *Your iniquities have turned away these things, and your sins have withholden good things from you.*

The Lord constantly blesses you, but you will miss seeing those blessings when you fellowship with evil.

3 John 2-4 *²Beloved, I wish above all things that thou mayest prosper and be in health, even as thy soul prospereth. ³For I rejoiced greatly, when the brethren came and testified of the truth that is in thee, even as thou walkest in the truth. ⁴I have no greater joy than to hear that my children walk in truth.*

We all face difficulties in this fallen world, and if your peace and joy is dependant on things going the way you think they should be, then you are an easy target for the devil.

Do you think the Lord Jesus went into self-pity when He was arrested and slandered and beaten and tortured before He died on that cross for all your sins?

Philippians 1:21-24 *²¹For to me to live is Christ, and to die is gain. ²²But if I live in the flesh, this is the fruit of my labour: yet what I shall choose I wot not. ²³For I am in a strait betwixt two, having a desire to depart, and to be with Christ; which is far better: ²⁴Nevertheless to abide in the flesh is more needful for you.*

Paul is resigning himself to whatever he had to face, and knowing what he knew by having such a personal encounter with the Lord Jesus, there was a pressure between staying here and living on earth, or dying and being with the Lord in Heaven. Translation: if it was just up to him, he would choose to go be with the Lord at this point and be in a much better place, but it is better he stay here a while longer for the church's sakes. Not a hint of self-pity in this, Paul is saying the Lord needs him here to help defend the faith and build the Kingdom; he needed to stay here and encourage the people with the Gospel.

In Colossians 1:23-24 *²³If ye continue in the faith grounded and settled, and be not moved away from the hope of the gospel, which ye have heard, and which was preached to every creature which is under heaven; whereof I Paul am made a minister; ²⁴Who now rejoice in my sufferings for you, and fill up that which is behind of the afflictions of Christ in my flesh for his body's sake, which is the church:*

Our Life as Believers is to Believe

Here is tremendous insight for us today. Again every thought you have must travel a pathway of Faith or Fear. Faith brings hope and the spirit of fear takes hope away.

The sufferings and afflictions are not diseases God is trying to teach you a lesson with. The sufferings and afflictions are just bumps in the road, and bumps are something you can climb onto to get higher and closer to Heaven.

We are all going to face problems that need to be resolved in this life. Just as someone who crossed over a creek to get to the other side, there are often stepping stones that can help you across.

Often times the problems we have to deal with and face in this life at the end of the day are nothing more than stepping stones to success in Christ. All the more reason you need to keep a heavenly perspective.

I mean after all, dead men like me are just happy to be alive in Christ.

Romans 6:11 *Likewise reckon ye also yourselves to be dead indeed unto sin, but alive unto God through Jesus Christ our Lord.*

Before Saul became the Apostle Paul, he was out there chasing down Christians and persecuting them, watching some of them get stoned to death like Stephen. Then the Lord in His perfect timing knocked Saul off his horse on the road to Damascus. I know the Lord is always a perfect gentlemen, so He must have caused Saul to come off his horse in a gentlemanly way as He knocked him down.

Sometimes people's hearts are so hardened, and in this case He must have needed to actually knock Saul off his horse to get his full-undivided attention. Other people are perhaps a bit more sensitive and He just needs to gently speak with them. God always knows the best way to get your attention.

How amazing it must have been when Saul fell off his horse and heard the Lord speak to him face to face in a blinding light. So much light must have overtaken him that he could not see. It was only when the Lord sent Ananias to pray and lay hands on him to be able to see again, that the scales not only fell off his natural eyes, but must have also opened his spiritual eyes.

Ephesians 1:18 *The eyes of your understanding being enlightened; that ye may know what is the hope of his calling, and what the riches of the glory of his inheritance in the saints,*

Papa God wants his children to understand and be in a close relationship with Him.

When you study Galatians you'll find that the Holy Spirit taught Paul for several years. Paul did not even meet Peter and John or any of the other Apostles for a number of years.

When the Lord had prepared Paul to meet the rest of the Apostles, they recognized the anointing on him and that the Holy Spirit had taught him and given him revelations. They ended up releasing him and commissioning Paul to go forward to reach the Gentiles. Peter and John must have been amazed how Paul had so many revelations and such knowledge as they did when they actually walked with Jesus in the flesh and Paul merely met Him after the resurrection.

I do not find any spirit of pride with Peter and John as Paul ends up starting more churches and writing more of the New Testament then they do. Not a trace of evil spirits of envy and jealousy, nor did they go into self-pity.

Peter and John were not complaining to the Lord by saying, "We spent all that time with You, how come You are giving this fellow Paul such favor?" Peter and John must have seen the "big picture" and realized that we all have different gifts as unique as fingerprints. They knew that the whole body works together, and you can not become envious of your arm doing its job, or your foot doing its job. You rejoice when the work is simply being done! We work together in the body of Christ as a body works together.

The Lord is bringing us together to take us into a higher level of understanding of who He really is.

The Lord Jesus spent 40 days fasting in the desert, and The Holy Spirit taught Paul through a similar type of experience. Once you get born again you step into a supernatural learning process, even if you must go through a dry desert type experience. After all, Moses did not even start in ministry until he was 80 years old!

The Apostle Paul said he had rejoiced in all the difficult things he had gone through, because he understood how it was meant for good and to help benefit the body of believers.

The moment you got saved as a believer, the enemy made you a target. You were previously working for the devil, and he was just using you anyway, and still hated you, but now the devil is at war with you.

Take your Rightful Place

Always remember: we are at war first in our thought life. However, if that spirit of self-pity has infiltrated you at this level, it will not let you go to fight in the war. That spirit of self-pity is going to hinder you from taking your rightful position in God's chosen army as a prince or princess warrior.

For example, anything in your life that not going right, instead of dealing with it, you give into it and accept thoughts like, "What is the use of trying, nothing ever works out right anyway," which is fear based and actually helps defend self-pity rather than use the supernatural weapons, equipment and amour the Lord gave you to battle against it.

2 Corinthians 11:23 *[11]Are they ministers of Christ?* (I speak as a fool) *I am more; in labours more abundant, in stripes above measure, in prisons more frequent, in deaths oft.* (Are we speaking as a madman, a fool, or the Gospel? In stripes above measure that in spite of the

opposition and being beaten in prisons more frequently then most he still presses on to bring the Gospel message.)

24Of the Jews five times received I forty stripes save one. (The Jews at this time did not repeat scourging except in great crimes but to Christians they apparently showed no mercy.) *25Thrice was I beaten with rods, once was I stoned, thrice I suffered shipwreck, a night and a day I have been in the deep;* (Acts 16:22 tells of these beatings) *26In journeyings often, in perils of waters, in perils of robbers, in perils by mine own countrymen, in perils by the heathen, in perils in the city, in perils in the wilderness, in perils in the sea, in perils among false brethren;*

27In weariness and painfulness, in watchings often, in hunger and thirst, in fastings often, in cold and nakedness. 28Beside those things that are without, that which cometh upon me daily, the care of all the churches. (He is saying besides all the outward sufferings there surely were many inward struggles because of the condition of the churches that were placed in Paul's care.)

29Who is weak, and I am not weak? who is offended, and I burn not? (The idea here is that no man is offended, but what if I were to burn with indignation?) *30If I must needs glory, I will glory of the things which concern mine infirmities.* (If I am going to boast I am going to tell about how I suffered to bring you the Gospel not on about how the Lord has equipped me with His power to lay hands on the sick so they recover which any believer can do)

31The God and Father of our Lord Jesus Christ, which is blessed for evermore, knoweth that I lie not.

How many true born again believers today would suffer for Christ? I mean would you really stand strong knowing your reward in Heaven awaits you, or would you end up in a prison cell in self-pity wanting to die? Would you be like John the Baptist in prison asking if

Jesus is really the Messiah or should we keep waiting for someone else?

At the end of the day, what it will really come down to is whether our faith based on feelings and allowing all the emotion's molecules to run havoc with our bodies, or is it based on truth and understanding of the Gospel?

Throughout the history of Christian Churches in America no one has had to suffer like that, because the American church has never really been persecuted. The media and television has actively worked on changing the image of Christians so that the secular world may see us as the enemy now—calling good evil and evil good. But so far, no one I have heard about has ever had to hide their Bibles from the secret police in America as they do in places like China. Not too many people in America have had to make the choice to go to prisons or to die, unless they deny the Gospel truth.

Why I am attacking/blaming/focusing on going after the spirit of self-pity so much is because it is a vile spirit and it is a sin entertained. It requires no faith whatsoever, and whatsoever is not of faith, is sin (Romans 14:23).

Romans 14:8 *For whether we live, we live unto the Lord; and whether we die, we die unto the Lord: whether we live therefore, or die, we are the Lord's.*

Let us keep our eternal heavenly perspective at all times, and stay in the Word, because faith comes by hearing the Word of our Lord, and because the spirit of self-pity uses the lies of the devil.

Besides, if you really want to prosper, I do not see anywhere in all the Bible that Papa God will impart to you new and creative ideas, and then bless you when you are still holding onto old toxic thinking. Holding on to those old nasty sinful ways of doing things, having a negative attitude murmuring and complaining about how you should be blessed and blaming others for your misfortunes. It would be best to just lie that stuff down and line up with the Holy Word so you can be blessed.

On the other side of that, I have observed that sometimes people will just keep being driven and striving to achieve something not understanding the devil is driving them, just as the Lord is trying to lead them in the other direction. Papa God may allow you to accomplish some things without His approval and His blessings, but then you will have to maintain that thing you did in your own strength and power, and that you may find not to be worth it in the end.

Prayer

Thank you, Lord, for leading us into all truth and righteousness before You. For giving us the confidence that whether we are awake or if we sleep we may look forward to uninterrupted fellowship with You all the time. Even now knowing we will be with you forever in all eternity. That every unclean spirit must go from us and that Your angels are encamped around us.

That we can pray without ceasing through the Holy Spirit. I ask Lord that we are able to decrease so that You may increase in all of us here and that signs and wonders do follow all of us in real tangible supernatural ways.

That we are to defeat the enemy of our souls by our faith and obedience to Your Word.

That we are not attached to this world and to our physical bodies, but that we can look forward to receiving our Glorified bodies. But in the meantime, I thank You for supernatural healing and miracles of the bodies we are in, that You heal Your people now. We thank You for supernatural provision for all our needs: emotionally, physically, financially and spiritually.

That we will not walk in ignorance of Your Word anymore, or of fear of any evil thing. But that we walk in Faith no matter how things may appear.

That we know we shall not die, but live with You forever, that the spirit of death can not have us, for whether we live, or die, we are the Lord's.

We thank You for helping us defeat the spirit of self-pity as we continue in Your Holy Word with a grateful heart. That we may enjoy the more abundant life You sent the Lord Jesus to provide for us.

We thank You Papa God in Jesus' Christ of Nazareth name, we pray. Amen.

Chapter 4

Blessings Come to Those Who Trust

In the last chapter I taught you, about being double-minded and how that means you're fighting on both sides of the battle. This makes you a double agent which brings a death sentence.

James 1:8 *A double minded man [is] unstable in all his ways.*

The wages and the payment of sin is death (Romans 6:23).

Now this is certainly not what the Lord wants for you, however, we have been given freedom of choice and it's up to you to decide moment by moment who you will obey, the Lord or the devil?

The Bible tells us in 3 John 1:2 *Beloved, I wish above all things that thou mayest prosper and be in health, even as thy soul prospereth.*

It seems just about everyone is seeking to walk in health and prosperity. And the good news is that indeed Papa God wants you to be healthy and prosper, but the key to understanding this appears to be that our souls must also be doing well. Even as thy soul prospereth.

What does that mean? It means that we understand that any unconfessed sin is hindering, or blocking us from our relationship with the Lord our God.

Some may define unconfessed sin as not recognizing or admitting it.

So any private unconfessed secret or hidden sin can separate us, denying us the promises of a God fulfilled life. Even if it happened a very long time ago, or if it seemed such a minor and subtle thing to us, it's not according to the Holy God that sees everything.

Jeremiah 5:25 *Your iniquities have turned away these things, and your sins have withholden good things from you.* (Sin withholds the good things God wants to bless you with.)

We need to stay Faithful. Luke 16:10 *He that is faithful in that which is least is faithful also in much: and he that is unjust in the least is unjust also in much.*

We have been bought and paid for by the very precious blood sacrifice of the Lamb of God Jesus Christ of Nazareth.

Revelation 4:11 *Thou art worthy, O Lord, to receive glory and honour and power: for thou hast created all things, and for thy pleasure they are and were created.*

This does not say we have been created for our own pleasure, but rather for the Lord's pleasure. This concept harmonizes with places where the Lord Jesus said things like:

Luke 22:42 *Father, if thou be willing, remove this cup from me: nevertheless not my will, but thine, be done.*

The Lord Jesus said very clearly here, not my will Father, but Your will be done, in my life, even if I must suffer a horrible death for the sake of this world and take on all their sins for all time.

Papa God is not asking you to do that, is He? However, the Lord Jesus has made it quite clear that if we love Him we need to keep His commandments no matter how we interpret the Grace message. Yes, we are saints, but a saint is simply a sinner saved by grace. His Mercy, grace and love, toward us is really undeserved favor. Grace is a measure of time to understand it and get right with Papa God. That is the sanctification process. His mercy and grace are undeserved because we remain guilty of sin, and we must not forget the wages of sin is always death (Romans 6:23).

If we say we love the Lord we still need to keep His

commandments.

John 15:10-17 *¹⁰If ye keep my commandments, ye shall abide in my love; even as I have kept my Father's commandments, and abide in his love. ¹¹These things have I spoken unto you, that my joy might remain in you, and that your joy might be full. ¹²This is my commandment, That ye love one another, as I have loved you. ¹³Greater love hath no man than this, that a man lay down his life for his friends. ¹⁴Ye are my friends, if ye do whatsoever I command you. ¹⁵Henceforth I call you not servants; for the servant knoweth not what his lord doeth: but I have called you friends; for all things that I have heard of my Father I have made known unto you. ¹⁶Ye have not chosen me, but I have chosen you, and ordained you, that ye should go and bring forth fruit, and that your fruit should remain: that whatsoever ye shall ask of the Father in my name, he may give it you. ¹⁷These things I command you, that ye love one another.*

If we could just get this one down, how blessed would we all be? Instead we often listen to those lying anti-Christ spirits that want to help us justify our sins. It is really amazing to me how quick most people seem to be in believing the worst about someone.

"A lie will travel halfway around the world before the truth even has a chance to get its pants on" ~ Sir Winston Churchill. He also said –"We make a living by what we get, but we make a life by what we give."

The Lord has blessed us with so many blessings and the more we give back unto Him the more we are blessed either here on earth or in Heaven, or both. We will be blessed as we decrease in self and allow the Holy Spirit to increase in us.

One of the reasons the Lord has me teaching and preaching so much here to expose that vile spirit of self-pity is probably because it's such a hard thing to see when you look in your mirror.

It is one of the craftiest spirits that seems to be able to hide behind so many faces. We must always test the spirits to see if they are from God or not, including a spirit of self-pity.

Always remember the devil himself can appear as an angel of light. What seems right, may not be right, it's up to us to know the difference. Some believe *pride* is a good thing... but it is not. It's the very thing that caused Satan to fall.

2 Corinthians 11:14 *And no marvel; for Satan himself is transformed into an angel of light.*

1 Peter 5:8 *Be sober, be vigilant; because your adversary the devil, as a roaring lion, walketh about, seeking whom he may devour:*

Looking in the Mirror

One of the hardest aspects when exposing the spirit of Self-pity in yourself is the mere recognition of it.

It is so deceptive and vile it can sometime bring a ministry session with a person suffering with self-pity to a complete halt. That spirit of self-pity will even have a person accuse the ministers and stand up and walk out saying something along the lines of "I can't listen to any more of this." They will refuse to deal with the real issues as to not expose the self-pity which is protecting all the other unclean, unholy spirits in the person.

They really appear like a Dr. Jekyll and Mr. Hyde depending on when the demons in them feel like manifesting.

The evil spirits in them are able to understand and they know if they allow the person to continue receiving ministry they will be forever cast out in Jesus name.

A person suffering like this in self-pity can actually think and claim with what they believe is being completely honest and transparent, in all earnestness that they really want to be healed and that they are really ready and willing to do whatever is required to get free. However, sadly no matter what way you seem to approach them that spirit of self-pity is going to try and block you from getting through to them. So until they recognize it and deal with it, nothing much will change and they will continue going down a pathway of destruction.

Because that spirit of self-pity in them is right there to distort the Gospel truth, it will act like it knows more than you, the person administering the Word of God to them by quoting the Scriptures.

They will also want you to stop quoting the Scriptures and say just talk to them as a person. They do not want to know that faith comes by the Word of God, because the spirit of fear needs them to manifest itself through.

They may even just plainly deny they have a problem all together, because they are so convinced there has to be someone else to blame for their suffering and it cannot be them as they are such a sainted person. So in the end it is basically down to this: you can do nothing more for someone who doesn't allow the Holy Spirit to work through them.

And so that person is not helped and they go off still very convinced that they are 'trying their best' but for some unknown reason no one ever understands them and God must have made a mistake ordaining that person as a minister or pastor who tried to help them.

They may even start to accuse those trying to help them by saying they are not a real Christian or a good person. They will attack the person who tries to help them as would a wild animal caught with one leg in a trap. They may viciously bite their rescuer in their torment and fear because they simply don't understand the truth.

The spirit of self-pity is blinding the individual of

seeing the truth about what is really going on. And as long as that spirit is there, this individual won't be able to see it either. So even though they want help, they aren't able to receive it. This spirit is very cunning and will even make it seem like they are getting free, only to manifest sometime during a ministry session, and close this persons eyes again to the Gospel Truth, leaving them where they started.

But there is good news, Papa God understands everything, and He will show us how to overcome everything, Our job is to look within and start being honest with ourselves and humbly come before Him.

There was a demon possessed man in Mark 5 who lived in a graveyard in the tombs crying out in torment and cutting himself, which is probably the same spirit of insanity that attacks people today who do such things. The demons recognized the Lord Jesus and the man who saw Jesus from a distance came running and fell at His feet to worship Him. Though this man was filled with many evil spirits there was still something good in him that allowed him to humble himself before the Lord which in return brought about his freedom.

Mark 5:6-9 *⁶But when he saw Jesus afar off, he ran and worshipped him, ⁷And cried with a loud voice, and said, What have I to do with thee, Jesus, thou Son of the most high God? I adjure thee by God, that thou torment me not. ⁸For he said unto him, Come out of the man, thou unclean spirit. ⁹And he asked him, What is thy name? And he answered, saying, My name is Legion: for we are many.*

A legion is 6,000! That is a lot of demons to have been in one person. This actually proves that they require little space to exist inside a person.

Then Jesus ended up commanding all the demons to come out of the man by sending them into a herd of swine which ran off a cliff and drowned making the first deviled ham recorded in history. Mind you, the evil spirits did not drown, they cannot be killed off like that because they are eternal spirit.

So, after receiving his freedom, this man who is now totally healed and in his right mind wants to travel with the Lord Jesus, but Jesus tells him to stay behind in that town and share what God has done for him. In other words, Jesus started a ministry and church through this formerly insane man. In today's churches, the most that this man would probably be in charge of is cleaning the parking lot. Unless, of course, you believe God can heal and totally change someone like Saul and make him into the Apostle Paul.

My point is that unless someone is willing to humble themselves before the Lord there is little you can do for them until they do.

In fact, the Scriptures tell us that sometimes you just have to turn someone over to let the devil "bless" them some more, and pray that at some point they will finally have had enough torment from the devil to truly seek the Lord's forgiveness, before it's too late.

1 Corinthians 5:5 *To deliver such an one unto Satan for the destruction of the flesh, that the spirit may be saved in the day of the Lord Jesus.*

2 Thessalonians 2:11 *And for this cause God shall send them strong delusion, that they should believe a lie:*

When you hear someone say, "Nobody really under-stands what I am going through. People are so insensi-tive to me all the time, what's wrong with them? Life has been so much harder for me than other people I know."

Then you can rest assure there is a spirit of self-pity operating in them.

They will also say things like, "No one really cares about me, no one ever calls me to see how I am doing." Which is usually spoken from a person who has worn most of their friends and other people out who have tried to come along and help them and love them, and because they are so stuck in that self-pity they aren't able to receive the help they need, but just blame others for not reaching out for them and coming to rescue them.

So they will claim it's entirely your fault for not trying harder to rescue them as they are lost in a sea of self-pity.

I have heard in years of ministry some people say things like, "I believe God heals people today, but only others, not me." I always asked them to show me in my Bible where it says that God will not heal them. That way I can avoid them showing me some modern translation that has watered down the Holy Word of God.

Then I usually tell them, "I agree with you, your absolutely right. God will not begin healing you as long as you continue to fellowship with devils and believe the devil's lies instead of the Gospel truth. It's really entirely your choice who you decide to obey and blessings or curses you decide to receive.

What vile lies does a person have to believe before that spirit of self-pity becomes a part of their thinking process to the point at which it takes on the same appearance of that person? Sometimes it masquerades itself to look like a spirit of righteousness.

One of the biggest issues of course is that all these spirits are quite invisible and the person suffering with them can't see them in themselves, just as you can not see germs, unless you use a high powered microscope, but then again that is why we have a Bible to use, because it is God's Holy microscope in a sense which exposes the devil and all his lies.

Those people around someone suffering with self-pity can see it pretty clearly at times because it has to manifest itself through the person to be able to express its fallen nature in words and actions.

When the devil took Scripture out of context and quoted it to the Lord Jesus in the time of his temptations, each time, Jesus simply and eloquently said with great authority, "it is written".

You really need to do the same thing. The devil knows the Bible really well as he has had thousands of years to study it, still greater is the Holy Spirit in you than any devil or demon.

You will do well to keep quoting and speaking the Word of God as the Lord gives us examples here. Besides, by mediating on the Word of God, it can heal you, (Proverbs 4:20-24) as it brings healing to all your flesh.

Matthew 4:1 *Then was Jesus led up of the Spirit into the wilderness to be tempted of the devil.* (If the Holy Spirit had to test Jesus as He tested Adam and people like Abraham and so many others, do you think you might be tested as well? Why should the Lord allow us to be with Him for all eternity if you won't obey Him here?

Verse 2, *"And when he had fasted forty days and forty nights, he was afterward an hungred."* Moses, Joshua and Elijah fasted this way, hunger always leaves after the first few days of a long fast when all the toxic poisons have been expelled from the body. (A healthy person can fast this long without harming themselves but must be careful to break the fast gradually and drink water throughout. Otherwise after 40 days starvation can set in.)

Verse 3 *And when the tempter came to him, he said, If thou be the Son of God, command that these stones be made bread.* This is a form of accusation which always comes from the devil; getting you to tempt God by not trusting His provision for you or that He really is your Heavenly Father.

Verse 4 *But he answered and said, It is written, Man shall not live by bread alone, but by every word that proceedeth out of the mouth of God.*

The Lord Jesus is only going to do what He sees His Father God doing and here he is actually quoting the Scripture back to the devil in proper context which was from Deuteronomy 8:3 *And he humbled thee, and suffered thee to hunger, and fed thee with manna, which thou knewest not, neither did thy fathers know; that he might make thee know that man doth not live by bread only, but by every word that proceedeth out of the mouth of the LORD doth man live.*

Matthew 4:5-8 *⁵Then the devil taketh him up into the holy city, and setteth him on a pinnacle of the temple, ⁶And saith unto him, If thou be the Son of God, cast thyself down: for it is written, He shall give his angels charge concerning thee: and in their hands they shall bear thee up, lest at any time thou dash thy foot against a stone. (here the devil misquoted the Bible to Jesus from Psalm 91:11-12) ⁷Jesus said unto him, It is written again, Thou shalt not tempt the Lord thy God.* (Jesus quoted Deuteronomy 6:16 here) *⁸Again, the devil taketh him up into an exceeding high mountain, and sheweth him all the kingdoms of the world, and the glory of them;*

Satan is the prince of this present world system since Adam ignorantly and foolishly handed it over to him, and what Satan wants the most is to have Jesus and everyone else completely surrender to him in submission and adoration, only that is not going to ever happen so help us God.

⁹And saith unto him, All these things will I give thee, if thou wilt fall down and worship me. ¹⁰Then saith Jesus unto him, Get thee hence, Satan: for it is written, Thou shalt worship the Lord thy God, and him only shalt thou serve.

(Jesus was basing this on Deuteronomy 6:13 *Thou shalt fear the LORD thy God, and serve him, and shalt swear by his name.)*

[11] Then the devil leaveth him, and, behold, angels came and ministered unto him. (the devil and demons will flee from us the same way as we stay obedient to Word of God and tell him to go)

James 4:7 *Submit yourselves therefore to God. Resist the devil, and he will flee from you. (*Hint hint, nudge nudge.)

As I was saying a bit earlier, the Apostle Paul tells us about things being rather difficult for him in 2 Corinthians Chapter 11, and how he was beaten unlawfully and then thrown into prison.

He was beaten five times by the Jews, and I am sure they did not show him any mercy. They had figured out that 40 stripes could kill a man so they more than likely stopped at 39 stripes as to keep him alive, leaving him suffering.

Three times Paul said he was beaten with rods. He was even left for dead once when they stoned him, and three times he was shipwrecked. It's hard to imagine being out on the sea all night and a day waiting on a rescue party to come and find you. It is hard enough today to do that with all the high technical advances made in search and recue. I imagine back then it was nearly impossible to locate someone lost at sea.

Paul also mentions the perils of being with thieves and robbers, as well as in perils of his own countrymen, along with all the heathens and their occultist practices.

I recall playing music in some places like that back in England. But at least they always offered you a cup of tea. However, it does not sound like that was the case here. Paul went on to tell us that he also experienced difficulties in the city, and troubles in the country and in the wilderness. He mentioned that among churches there were false brethren—people pretending to be born again believers who were not—and they were used by the enemy to go out to harm him and the name of the Lord.

Sadly, I'm sure we have met a few people like that along the way.

So here is Paul, he must have been weary from well doing, in pain from all the beatings, in hunger and thirst at times. Paul says quite often he was cold and suffered in nakedness, and we think we are having a bad day when the car or refrigerator breaks down.

As Paul did, we need to give thanks for all things and believe that perhaps it was a blessing in disguise. What do most people do? What do you do? Do you react as a child of God or a child of this present world system?

Obedience is Key

Exodus 19:5-6 *⁵Now therefore, if ye will obey my voice indeed, and keep my covenant, then ye shall be a peculiar treasure unto me above all people: for all the earth is mine: ⁶And ye shall be unto me a kingdom of priests, and an holy nation. These are the words which thou shalt speak unto the children of Israel.*

I do not find any scripture in the Bible that even hints that Paul entertained a spirit of self-pity, even with all the trials he went through. It seems he was much too busy sharing the Gospel and leading people to Christ to have time to bother entertaining a spirit of self-pity. That might be a key to our own understanding of how to avoid such traps of the devil.

If you are really going to defeat the spirit of self-pity, you must first humble yourself before the Lord, then get into a place of being grateful and thankful—the opposite of the spirit of self–pity.

When this happens you can ask the Holy Spirit to come and assist you by yanking that evil thing out in the all mighty name of Jesus Christ of Nazareth. Finally, that thing has to go from you into the dry place.

Matthew12:43 *When the unclean spirit is gone out of a man, he walketh through dry places, seeking rest, and findeth none.*

Often an evil spirit will leave willingly on its own because once you know the truth the truth makes you free (John 8:31-32). It is this concept that justifies sharing the Word.

I confronted someone one day who was concerned and fearful about all these laboratory tests she got back accompanied by negative doctor's reports. I suggested she read my book called, "What Was I Thinking?" and gain some knowledge of how our body and thoughts work.

She said, "How can reading help me recover from this sickness?" I countered by reminding her why the Lord gave us Scriptures like...

Proverbs 4:20-22 *20My son, attend to my words; incline thine ear unto my sayings. 21Let them not depart from thine eyes; keep them in the midst of thine heart. 22For they are life unto those that find them, and health to all their flesh.*

Or Psalm 107:20 *He sent his word, and healed them, and delivered them from their destructions.*

Yes, indeed the Word of God can heal you. Once your mind accepts God's Holy truth the rest of you will catch up and healing will happen as you leave the devil's lies behind you.

Let's take an example from the words of Jesus, "Get behind me Satan" and I'll add "get out of my way in Jesus name."

In the study of Epigenetics (the study of heritable changes in gene expression or cellular phenotype) which actually reveals things the Bible said all along, there are quite a few scientific studies that show how your thoughts, beliefs and emotions can actually alter even your genes, which in turn affect your health and your perceptions to a greater or lesser degree, depending on the thoughts produced.

This is why you must learn to think about what you are thinking about and think Holy thoughts. If you stay in faith, blessings will truly follow. Don't let any spirit, including self-pity, have any place in you to poison your genetic make up.

Papa God knows everything and He still has a great plan and purpose for your life. You may not understand everything you are going through right now, but lift up your arms and praise Him for who He is. No matter what you may be going through right now, no matter how many disappointments you may be suffering, when you stay in faith, blessings will happen. Scriptures say that without faith it is impossible to please Him.

No matter how many times things don't go the way you think they should and you are feeling disappointed, don't lose your joy for the Lord.

If you've been knocked down, get back up. Papa God sees your faith and He sees your determination to please Him and do what is right in His sight as He sees everything. When you've done all you can do, that's when God will do what you can't do.

Ephesians 6:13 *Wherefore take unto you the whole armour of God, that ye may be able to withstand in the evil day, and having done all, to stand.*

So often you have heard people give many different excuses why they can't get something accomplished. Or they say they will help someone out when they are not so depressed. Depression can accompany a spirit of self-pity, and it is a spirit of heaviness the Lord certainly did not give you. It's evil and it needs to be evicted in Jesus' name. Then that person needs to get on with the assignment the Lord has given all of His children. We need to get to work here because we were all bought with a price.

In fact, it says when you help bless others, when you help share the Gospel and help people recognize those places they fell into sin and how to walk in obedience and faith. God will bless you when you help feed and clothe the poor and cover them, even your own healing will speed up for you.

Isaiah 58:7-8 *⁷Is it not to deal thy bread to the hungry, and that thou bring the poor that are cast out to thy house? when thou seest the naked, that thou cover him; and that thou hide not thyself from thine own flesh? ⁸Then shall thy light break forth as the morning, and thine health shall spring forth speedily: and thy righteousness shall go before thee; the glory of the LORD shall be thy reward.*

Truly Papa God is more interested in how we look on the inside than the outside. He is able to mend our broken hearts, so as we grow in our relationship with Him, and continually interact with His Holy Spirit, the sanctification process unfolds. Our obedience will even manifest out of that relationship. This is what it means when the scriptures say, *we show our faith by our works*, which is how it is supposed to be.

Matthew 5:13-16 *¹³Ye are the salt of the earth: but if the salt have lost his savour, wherewith shall it be salted? it is thenceforth good for nothing, but to be cast out, and to be trodden under foot of men.*

¹⁴Ye are the light of the world. A city that is set on an hill cannot be hid. We are supposed to let our lights shine as believers from the inside out. It's like someone driving down the road and seeing a major city all lit up.

¹⁵Neither do men light a candle, and put it under a bushel, but on a candlestick; and it giveth light unto all that are in the house. ¹⁶Let your light so shine before men, that they may see your good works, and glorify your Father which is in heaven.

We are to help glorify the Lord by sharing the Gospel, healing the sick, and casting out demons in Jesus name. Have you ever seen anyone suffering with a spirit of self-pity doing that? No. They are too occupied blaming others and complaining about their own lives and how other people have let them down.

The Lord Jesus must be our example. He was emotionally slandered, lied about in court and accused, yet he did not answer his accusers and neither should you. They physically beat Him and inhumanely nailed Him to a cross. Nowhere do we find in Scripture where He is entertaining any spirit of self-pity, even as He was in excruciating pain and suffering. He even led one of the criminals next to him into salvation when the criminal recognized that Jesus must truly be the Messiah.

I think it was fitting that He was crucified between two prisoners, as one repents and is saved and the other one dies with his harden heart, showing us we have freedom of choice. One goes into paradise, even though he did not have time to be discipled and baptized a true death-bed-type of conversion, and the other thief goes into eternal hell fire with all his bitterness and memories of life on earth.

As our Lord Jesus was suspended in great agony on that cross, just before he is about to die, he was asking Father God in Heaven to forgive them, for they don't know what they were doing.

Isn't it time we learn this lesson and get free, by forgiving everyone, including ourselves now?

Martin Luther was quoted as saying, "You are responsible not only for what you say, but also for what you do not say."

Prayer

Please read the following prayer out loud, so that both kingdoms hear your proclamation.

Papa God, I come before you now in the name of our Lord and Savior Jesus Christ of Nazareth, the Messiah Yeshua, just as You instructed us to do in Hebrews 4:16 *Let us therefore come boldly unto the throne of grace, that we may obtain mercy, and find grace to help in time of need.*

Lord I want you to show me if there is any self-pity in me. I don't want to be deceived by that evil spirit, as I may not even know it is there. I give you permission to expose it, and remove it from my life. Help me to cooperate with you as you do this, and not fall into fear when you begin to work on that area. From this teaching, I need to be aware of that spirit's tactics, not to be ignorant of his devices any longer, so that I'm not taken captive of the enemy at his will. I want to see the Truth, I want to be freed from this.

I ask you to help me to remain in faith and not fall into fear when you begin dealing with me in this area. I thank you for your help and healing.

I thank you Papa God for using this booklet to work out of me that which is in me, to become a clean vessel, holy and sanctified so that I am fit for your use when you call.

I also confess anything that has hindered me from having my prayers answered. I choose to forgive everyone who has offended me and hurt me in any way in my life and on both sides of my generations all the way back to Adam. So that I may now receive and fully accept Your forgiveness in your almighty mercy, grace and love.

That as I confess my sins, You are willing to again

wash me clean from all filthiness of the flesh and spirit. I believe that You are faithful and just to forgive me of my sins, and to cleanse me from all unrighteousness.

(Now take a moment and name off any sins)

Lord I thank You for forgiving me and I want to continue to walk in the light, your glorious light and to walk humbly before my Lord and have fellowship with You always. I also want to continue to fellowship with one another, so that the blood of Jesus Christ Your only begotten Son cleanses me from all sin.

That through the sacrifice of Jesus on the cross, I have passed out from under the curse and entered into the blessings of Abraham, whom You blessed in all things. The Word says that no weapon formed against a true spirit–filled born again believer shall prosper, and every tongue that rises against any in judgment is already condemned. I believe this is our heritage, our inherited right, as Your adopted children and Your friends and servants. That my righteousness is in You, O Lord. according to Isaiah 54:17.

Lord, now that I have forgiven all who have spoken evil against me, and having forgiven them, I now bless them in the all powerful name of Jesus Christ of Nazareth from my heart. That you lay not these charges against them but that they be saved and converted, as I know that you do not want any to perish. I thank You Papa God that I am in Christ, and therefore I am a new creation. All those old things have passed away and every thing in my life continues to become new. In Jesus Christ of Nazareth's Name, Amen.

2 Corinthians. 5:17-18 *17Therefore if any man be in Christ, he is a new creature: old things are passed away; behold, all things are become new. 18And all*

things are of God, who hath reconciled us to himself by Jesus Christ, and hath given to us the ministry of reconciliation.

Chapter 5

The Fight For Our lives

As I have mention before, the new science of Epigenetics studies are showing that those extra-cellular factors that influence genetic expression and personalities are only confirming the Holy Bible from my perspective. We've been told this all along in places like in Exodus 34:7 that's says our fathers sins and iniquities can come upon our children's children, unto the third and the fourth generation. So your thought life not only affects you, but now science is showing us it also affects your children and your great, great grandchildren as the Bible told us!

So Science is now showing that your parents and ancestor's thought lives, and all their life experiences, from the decisions they made moment to moment when they obeyed the Lord and when they disobeyed the Lords commandments, have somehow even affected you. In fact, this has somehow altered the eggs and sperm with that information and actually rewrote it in a way that changed some genetic codes indelibly that are then passed onto their children up to the third and fourth generations.

Listen, if the devil is able to do this, then certainly God is able to put things back in you they way He designed it to be.

The changing of genetic code, which is scientifically called 'transgenerational epigenetic inheritance,' is showing that something outside the cell is influencing it and altering things by turning on and off certain controls and switches on the genes. That means things that are outside of physical strengths and diet, and environments, or the way you are brought up is effecting and controlling the way the genes of the DNA behave in the sperm and eggs. In other words, the way you live your life is leaving a very definite imprint on the lives you help bring into this world. If you are guided by the Holy Spirit, you and your offspring will be blessed. If you are guided by other unclean spirits from the devils kingdom, they will bring curses to you and through you.

Deuteronomy 28 sums it up by saying that if we obey the Lord we will be blessed, and if we don't, sin opens the door for the enemy to bring curses into our lives.

Genesis 4:7 *If thou doest well, shalt thou not be accepted? and if thou doest not well, sin lieth at the door. And unto thee shall be his desire, and thou shalt rule over him.*

Right there it says, "sin lieth at the door," in other words waiting to get in. For example, a symptom is like sin trying to enter in. A spirit of fear will open that door for sickness and diseases and problems to come in.

How wonderful it is to know the Lord tells us this in places like Psalm 103:1-3 *1Bless the LORD, O my soul: and all that is within me, bless his holy name. 2Bless the LORD, O my soul, and forget not all his benefits: 3Who forgiveth all thine iniquities; who healeth all thy diseases;*

This must be one good reason why God created repentance—so we could use it! He knows we aren't perfect and we might fall into sin from time to time.

Some of us need to stop being so hard on ourselves and take our peace back by simply trusting in the Lord and walking in faith. This is a narrow path of holiness we walk; it is not a tight rope that God asked us to walk, that would be what a spirit of religion and legalism would have you to believe.

When I was initially doing some research for the idea of writing "What Was I Thinking?" I discovered many scientific ideas that did not line up with the Bible. One such idea, of how our minds and bodies work, dispels that old idea that intellectual limits are set in childhood and after about 25 years of age you start to decline from there.

The Bible says we as believer's are being changed daily as a work of the Holy Spirit.

2 Corinthians 3:18 *But we all, with open face beholding as in a glass the glory of the Lord, are changed into the same image from glory to glory, even as by the Spirit of the Lord.*

Science is getting a better grasp of studying the brain, and in recent years they have discovered how your state of mind can actually greatly influence your overall mental and physical health. Naturally, this was in the Bible all along.

Proverbs 23:7 *For as he thinketh in his heart, so is he: Eat and drink, saith he to thee; but his heart is not with thee.*

The good news is that with God all things are possible even increasing your IQ score. Which also means there are no limits with the Lord for your life. The sky is the limit.

For example, science cannot prove there are virgin births. If we locked up several test studies of virgins for nine months, it is highly unlikely they would produce babies. Furthermore, no one I know of has divided the Red Sea since Moses did in an emergency situation as the Israelites were facing.

Many of the miracles we read of in the Bible cannot be proven by today's scientific methods because they are supernatural. We see many supernatural healings and miracles today because God will not change who He is. He is still performing them as He has over the centuries and decides how and who as we obey His commandments. Because His Word will not change but it can help change us.

Hebrews 13:8 *Jesus Christ the same yesterday, and to day, and for ever.*

Malachi 3:6 *For I am the LORD, I change not; therefore ye sons of Jacob are not consumed.*

Using Your Brain

I suppose the most astounding information that science is showing in some of its newest research is that the brain continues to grow and change no matter what age you are; as it really all depends on *how you use your brain.*

One of the biggest problems with the invention of television seems to be how it has altered the use of imagination, which consequently brought about the computer age. As the images are doing so much of the imagination for you as opposed to reading a book or hearing the sounds like words and music would. As Faith comes by hearing and hearing the Word of God, it releases the truth into your imaginations. The enemy has gotten rather adept at performing this process in reverse with similar results.

Your imagination is so powerful that God had to change and divide people into many different languages at the tower of Babble and then divide continents as well.

Genesis 11:6 *And the LORD said, Behold, the people is one, and they have all one language; and this they begin to do: and now nothing will be restrained from them, which they have imagined to do.*

2 Corinthians 10:5 *Casting down imaginations, and every high thing that exalteth itself against the knowledge of God, and bringing into captivity every thought to the obedience of Christ;*

When you spend time studying the Word of God, it can become an intense time of mental focus as the Word of God is like fresh manna from heaven everyday.

So as you are receiving new revelations and insights and you are literally "switching on" what science terms neuroplasticity, you are also recognizing that you were fearfully and wonderfully made and designed to live forever. You have this amazing ability in your brain to continue to grow healthy branches of thoughts in a limitless unending unfolding of networks to continually increase your intelligence.

I was reflecting the other day from my own experiences how I have heard doctors say that they did not want to give anyone "false hope." So they often tell them the worst case scenario. Perhaps that is something lawyers came up with which is now taught in medical schools?

This could be why Shakespeare wrote his famous quote from King Henry VI "The first thing we do, let's kill all the lawyers'.

You need to give people hope for, without hope, people will die.

Even lawyers need hope; they are people too. Some are good who listen to truth others listen to the wrong kingdom. That reminds me about the two lawyers who brought their own sandwiches into a Pub in England and each ordered a drink. The owner sees them and comes over and says, "Just a minute here, you gents cannot come in here bringing your own sandwiches and eat them in my Pub." So the two lawyers looked at each other, shrugged and exchanged sandwiches.

The Bible tells us that hope is like an anchor for our soul and spirit. That Faith is the substance of things HOPED for. Hope is necessary to help boast your immune system when you have compromised it somewhere. I think faith and hope are very important to receiving healing. Your faith and your hope trump every unclean spirit of doubt and unbelief.

How many times did Jesus say to someone, "According to your faith let it be done unto you?" He said this when He healed the blind person found in Matthew 9:29 *Then touched he their eyes, saying, According to your faith be it unto you.*

There are so many amazing testimonies in the Bible and so many amazing testimonies today. And by sharing our testimonies, we are defeating the enemy.

Revelation 12:11 *And they overcame him by the blood of the lamb and the word of their testimony and loved not their lives unto the death.*

I have read and studied about people who were in accidents and suffered severe trauma to the brain, but instead of being like a vegetable, as the doctors predicted, they ended up being totally healed by the Lord and even continued to achieve intellectual abilities no one thought possible. With God all things are possible!

What about people who suffered with depression (a spirit of heaviness) who were delivered and went on to achieve wonderful things in the name of the Lord. I recall hearing about a man who retired as a airline pilot who went back to college and became an accountant at 80 years old!

Well Moses did not even start in ministry until he was 80 years old.

What you *think* will strengthen or weaken neural pathways as long as you live. After that, you will still have all the memories and continue learning in the next world depending where you spend eternity.

Strategies to Follow

Any good General must understand the enemy and develop strategies to win the battles and the war. What about all of us who are called to be ambassadors of Christ as born again Christians?

2 Corinthians 5:20 *Now then we are ambassadors for Christ, as though God did beseech you by us: we pray*

you in Christ's stead, be ye reconciled to God.

Studying the Bible helps us develop strategic approaches to how we think, which necessitates an understanding of who we are as children of God and which of our gifts are to be used for His Glory.

So how we are trained to think, is vital to our well being, as we study and renew our minds to the Word of God, the Holy Spirit is training us how to think. This will create new neural pathways in your brain as you accept the Word of God in your hearts which will also strengthen existing ones for as long as you live! As Christians, we will live forever.

The reverse is also true if you allow the devil and his army of demons to train you in unrighteousness with a spirit of fear and unforgiveness. This is why the Lord tells us to think about good things in Philippians 4:7-8 *And the peace of God, which passeth all understanding, shall keep your hearts and minds through Christ Jesus. *Finally, brethren, whatsoever things are true, whatsoever things are honest, whatsoever things are just, whatsoever things are pure, whatsoever things are lovely, whatsoever things are of good report; if there be any virtue, and if there be any praise, think on these things.*

So in other words, how you have been trained to think, and what you are thinking, can greatly affect you and your life.

When you are more concerned about me, myself and I than you are about the Word of God, there is a problem. That is self-pity at it's best... it is idolatry, and it is a sin.

How we think and how our thinking affects us emotionally and physically is certainly now being proven and revealed scientifically to show what the Lord has said all along throughout the Holy Bible—that our thought life has more influence over our genes than diet and exercise. Again, it is not so much what you eat, but rather what's eating you.

It is your Choice

You are the one that Papa God put in charge of your body—your Holy Temple. You are not a victim of biology or chance, you are able to learn the Gospel and be an overcomer.

The truth is that how and what we think, influences every aspect of who we are and how we perceive the world, and how we feel physically.

I read about a recent study written in the journal of Psychosomatic Medicine that stress, which is really a spirit of fear that God did not give you, can slow the healing of wounds by as much as 40%, as reduce by two-thirds the production of one cytokine—interleukin-1—that is integral for the healing process.

Again, confirming that as we consider a spirit of fear, stress and anxiety is really your body's reaction to your thought life, you are in fact helping to create your state of mind, which can be quite detrimental to your mental and physical health.

So in other words, every thought you don't capture to the obedience of Christ, can be very dangerous to your well being. Because your thoughts actually encompass all your belief systems and then dictate your feelings. What you believe will then create and establish a state of continuous health or continuous problems from those evil toxic thoughts that bring sickness and dis-ease.

When you see someone full of the joy of the Lord, you will find a body of health. However, someone without the joy of the Lord you will find unhappiness and chronic health and relationship problems. It's the truth isn't it?

No matter how sick or mentally challenged we may feel, we still have freedom of choice. We still have the ability to choose what thoughts and feelings we will allow ourselves to entertain and dwell with. Papa God has given us His Word to guide us, to heal us, and equip each one of us with all the spiritual and genetic material we need. He has given us the epigenetic ability to deal optimally with all the challenges that life in this world may bring.

At the end of the day it comes down to this found in Deuteronomy 30:19-20 *¹⁹I call heaven and earth to record this day against you, that I have set before you life and death, blessing and cursing: therefore choose life, that both thou and thy seed may live: ²⁰That thou mayest love the LORD thy God, and that thou mayest obey his voice, and that thou mayest cleave unto him: for he is thy life, and the length of thy days: that thou mayest dwell in the land which the LORD sware unto thy fathers, to Abraham, to Isaac, and to Jacob, to give them.*

The Lord has made each one of us with unique talents and gifts. as you are the only "you" there will ever be. Each one of us is a marvelous creation.

Psalm 139:14 *I will praise thee; for I am fearfully and wonderfully made: marvellous are thy works; and that my soul knoweth right well.*

1 Peter 4:10-11 *¹⁰As every man hath received the gift, even so minister the same one to another, as good stewards of the manifold grace of God. ¹¹If any man speak, let him speak as the oracles of God; if any man minister, let him do it as of the ability which God giveth: that God in all things may be glorified through Jesus Christ, to whom be praise and dominion for ever and ever. Amen.*

Papa God has given all of us different gifts to use for the purpose of His pleasure and to build up the kingdom of God. Let us pray then to discern how we can release the power God has within us each day. Personally I think that releasing God's power is part of the sanctification process that continues to develop as we grow and mature in the gifts He has given us.

The more I studied and practiced my guitar, the easier it became to express musical ideas on it.

If we want to experience the fullness of life, we must allow God's power to be released through us, even though we are not walking a perfect line as much as we may want to. There was a time, after the Lord performed a miracle and healed me from a so called incurable heart disease, that I felt I was walking a tight rope trying to be so careful not to sin anywhere. Then the Lord in His mercy, grace and love took me aside and explained that He did not call us to walk a tight rope of holiness, but rather a narrow path of Holiness. On a narrow path, there is still room for the Holy Spirit and other saints to walk with you.

Matthew 7:13-14 *13Enter ye in at the strait gate: for wide is the gate, and broad is the way, that leadeth to destruction, and many there be which go in thereat: 14Because strait is the gate, and narrow is the way, which leadeth unto life, and few there be that find it.*

The truth is, most of us do not take every single of our 30,000 to 70,000 thoughts a day captive to the obedience of Christ. But as we practice doing this, we will keep improving. The Lord sees in our hearts that we want to do the right things and we want to please Him and stay in faith and not sin by fearing anything.

Besides, the Lord would certainly not have told us to take every thought we have each day captive to the obedience of Christ unless we could practice doing that.

He knows we have all fallen short of His glory which is why He sent the Lord Jesus to cover us as believers in His precious blood. We are able to repent as we discern and recognize those places we are not lining up with the Word of God. We want to be perfect as Christ is, but we are not, this side of Heaven.

Our spirits are made clean and brand new as we were born again, but all of us still have to be transformed, which is the sanctification process.

Sometimes I have wondered if when the Lord Jesus walked here on earth did He ever got things like blisters from his sandals, or even blisters and cuts as a carpenter? Did He experience any pain in his body from sleeping on the ground with the Apostles? It seems to me that if He did, I am guessing He did not focus on those things, but on His Father God and thus carried on walking by His Holy Spirit.

We know there were times when He was hungry and thirsty in the "natural" but He continued to walk in the "Spirit."

There was a woman at the well He encountered in John 4 who He asked to give Him a drink of water and then ended up revealing to her who He was.

John 4:13-14 *[13]Jesus answered and said unto her, Whosoever drinketh of this water shall thirst again: [4]But whosoever drinketh of the water that I shall give him shall never thirst; but the water that I shall give him shall be in him a well of water springing up into everlasting life.*

We are told in John 4:24 *God is a Spirit: and they that worship him must worship him in spirit and in truth.*

Galatians 5:18 *But if ye be led of the Spirit, ye are not under the law.*

So let us keep walking in the spirit and in truth, and understand, whether we live or whether we die, we are the Lord's.

Romans 14:8 *For whether we live, we live unto the Lord; and whether we die, we die unto the Lord: whether we live therefore, or die, we are the Lord's.*

We just need to master being very conscientious with our thoughts and our words, and continue to check to see if it is edifying or not, before we utter a word.

Personally I think that when you simply start thinking about ungodly things, it may be like a drop of blood in the ocean and it will attract the sharks to come find you. When you entertain ungodly thinking, it may attract the demonic realm to launch an attack, at which time we are going to have to fight the good fight of Faith. The Bible tells us, when you have done all you know to do just stand, but I don't think that means stand around doing nothing, it means stand being prepared and ready for the next battle. Understand the rules of engagement.

Ephesians 6:13 *Wherefore take unto you the whole armour of God, that ye may be able to withstand in the evil day, and having done all, to stand.*

That means you have submitted to the Lord, resisting the devil, and he will eventually flee, unless you start questioning the orders you have been given. Why does the Christian army so often seem to question God; no other type of soldiers would ever do that?

Matthew 6:25 *Therefore I say unto you, Take no thought for your life, what ye shall eat, or what ye shall drink; nor yet for your body, what ye shall put on. Is not the life more than meat, and the body than raiment?*

God Still Heals Today

We must not live under the stigma of any labels. The devil brings diseases and problems, but we do not need to accept those things or believe we need to live with them the rest of our lives. There are too many documented testimonies now where even people born with disabilities have been healed of the Lord. Be mindful with your words that have great power in them, don't be claiming ownership of diseases and problems just because you are dealing with them.

A sister in Christ that I have spoken with a number of times over the years had to face years of cruelty and tortures by the enemy of our soul. She weighed less than two pounds at birth, and soon developed cerebral palsy, a disorder that left her crippled. Then her parents died in a motorcycle accident when she was 1 year old. She grew up a spastic quadriplegic and pretty much depended on other people to provide for her most basic needs. She needed someone to help her get in and out of bed, in and out of her wheelchair, and to help her go to the toilet.

She didn't have any control of her head or her neck and the medical community did not think there was much hope for her recovery." Then one day God showed her a vision of seeing herself out riding a bike on beautiful green grass. She believed Romans 4:17, calling things that are not as though they are. Three weeks later she ended up in a church service where there were only 7 people present who dared to believe the Gospel really worked, and she was totally healed. She got out of that wheel chair and ran about the church. God had performed a miracle.

Today she runs a flower shop, rides her bicycle, and testifies to the Great Physician Messiah Yeshua Jesus Christ of Nazareth Jehovah Rapha our healer. What if she entertained a spirit of self–pity? She might have never been healed. But she believed the Word of God, and what God does for one person, He will do for others who seek Him with their whole hearts.

The devil and his demons do all they can to try and block us from achieving all God has and wants for us, so we must learn to beat him at his own game by applying the truth of the Word of God in our everyday lives. God has given us important gifts to use. I am not talking about playing a musical instrument or being clever in the Arts and Sciences or sport and public speaking. I mean those spiritual gifts that are just waiting to be unleashed and to be used and blessed by the Lord. When you trust in the Word of God, all things are possible.

Don't Worry, Be Happy!

Each one of us is a work in progress and we all have a unique way that we process information, which helps us to think things through. The way you think and see the world is something you can do that no one else can do. This is a special gift the Lord puts in each one of us. Just like having different fingerprints.

The Lord tells us throughout the Bible in places like Proverbs 4:5 *Get wisdom, get understanding: forget it not; neither decline from the words of my mouth.*

So it appeared to me as I studied the Word of God, you really are in control of what you think. The Word of God teaches us to think properly, and if you do, you will become someone very useful in helping to bring some heaven to earth. You will be blessed as we learn to think about things in a Godly way with a Heavenly perspective.

As we practice, we will learn to discern what voices are trying to speak in our thoughts through Theta brain waves. That way we will only entertain those thoughts that line up with the Holy Scriptures.

If we can work towards that goal, we may even lighten up, laugh, and smile more! It's quite good for your health.

Proverbs 15:13 *A merry heart maketh a cheerful countenance: but by sorrow of the heart the spirit is broken.*

Proverbs 17:22 *A merry heart doeth good like a medicine: but a broken spirit drieth the bones.*

Papa God knows what He is talking about and there are some fabulous neurological effects that benefit us from smiling. Just the mere act of smiling can help stop and prevent those evil spirits from trying to set up a negative toxic mindset in you. Some of the latest medical research is showing that smiling actually helps with the rewiring of certain circuits in your brain that helps you maintain a positive out look and attitude about your life!

Smiling, like raising your eyebrows in surprised laughter or lowering them in anger, is a universal expression understood by all humans. It seems even my horse and dog can understand it! Basically smiling will make you feel happier and even help improve intelligence. This occurs because God designed us in such a way that when joy is triggered, the part of our brain that is involved with helping us make good decisions is released. That part of us, that pursues the intellectual and rational areas, is actually strengthened by smiling.

Some of the latest medical research shows that smiling may actually help lower blood pressure because you are not entertaining the spirit of fear as you smile, which also helps stimulate your immune system. Do you think if God designed us with freedom of choice that our brains would be triggering switches on and off by signals and cues being transmitted from our perceptions and body which help determine our moods and emotions?

For example, when someone sincerely smiles at you, how does that affect you? It's almost contagious, and causes you to smile back, causing your brain to release some of those feel good chemicals like Dopamine, and Serotonin, bringing joy to your spirit. The reverse is also true. When someone frowns and disapprovingly looks at you, it could release all those toxic chemicals which are the ingredients for sickness and diseases.

If smiling and laughing have such a profound affect maybe we need to be practicing this more. In places like London and New York, you soon learn not to make eye contact with people on the street because they might take you for a tourist and try to take advantage of you.

However, as a believer full of the joy of the Lord, it seems to be a good idea to practice sharing a smile and then observe how the Lord will use that as you watch and feel the responses of those who return a smile to you.

There was this Frenchman named Duchenne, who went about in the mid 1800's poking and zapping peoples faces in a seemingly mad attempt to figure out whether or not the muscles of the face were somehow connected to the persons soul.

He was unable to find what he was searching for but did discover that the eye muscles were hard to control and conceal as apart of involuntary smiling. He ended up collecting a huge amount of data about human facial muscles, which modern researchers have built upon. So in fact, you can tell a real smile from an attempted one because the eyes give it away. We have all heard the eyes are the windows to the soul which probably comes from this as the the Lord tells us in Matthew 6:22-23 *²²The light of the body is the eye: if therefore thine eye be single, thy whole body shall be full of light. ²³But if thine eye be evil, thy whole body shall be full of darkness. If therefore the light that is in thee be darkness, how great is that darkness!*

I think sometime we as believers just need to simply trust that Papa God loves us and has a good plan for us to help us escape whatever the enemy is trying to do.

When things don't make sense to you, just know that they always do to Papa God. He is not up in Heaven sitting on His throne concerned about how this is all going to work out. He already knows the beginning to the end.

His plans are more complex and higher than our plans. Most of the time we are only really seeing with our natural eyes until we spend time with Him and in His Word and He starts to show us things the way He sees them.

God is orchestrating things to bless us; He is not going to use manipulation, ever.

Manipulation is part of the spirit of self-pity and that is evil. Maybe as part of God's army we will do better to just receive our marching orders and march, so those walls trying to prevent us from moving forward in our life simply come tumbling down like they did in the story of Jericho. Imagine patiently marching around a city seven times, and when the signal was given they shout praise to God blowing trumpets and receiving the promise. You can read about it in Joshua Chapter 6. I expect they were smiling and joyful.

Let me take you to Acts 20:22 *²²And now, behold, I go bound in the spirit unto Jerusalem, not knowing the things that shall befall me there: ²³Save that the Holy Ghost witnesseth in every city, saying that bonds and afflictions abide me. ²⁴But none of these things move me, neither count I my life dear unto myself, so that I might finish my course with joy, and the ministry, which I have received of the Lord Jesus, to testify the gospel of the grace of God.*

Sometimes we just need to march on following the Lord even though we can see some trouble ahead of us.

If you are more concerned about your own self then about the Lord, or you are attracted to the things of this world, that is a problem that needs to be settled.

1 John 2:15 *Love not the world, neither the things that are in the world. If any man love the world, the love of the Father is not in him.*

Luke 17:32-33 *³²Remember Lot's wife. ³³Whosoever shall seek to save his life shall lose it; and whosoever shall lose his life shall preserve it.*

Luke 9:24 *For whosoever will save his life shall lose it: but whosoever will lose his life for my sake, the same shall save it.*

A spirit of pride wants to keep us in this world to eventually destroy us. Expressing a spirit of humility and a grateful heart is the way that leads to blessings in Christ. We must finish this race with the joy of our Lord in His mercy, grace and love.

Let me walk you through Hebrews 12 starting in Verse 1 *Wherefore seeing we also are compassed about with so great a cloud of witnesses, let us lay aside every weight, and the sin which doth so easily beset us, and let us run with patience the race that is set before us.* (The apostle Paul is saying here lay aside any things that weight you down such as a spirit of self-pity and bitterness because that is a sin)

Verse 2 *Looking unto Jesus the author and finisher of our faith; who for the joy that was set before him endured the cross, despising the shame, and is set down at the right hand of the throne of God.* (The Joy of the Lord is so powerful that Jesus was willing to endure the cross for the greater good of all, and without complaint, because it was the Father's will.)

Verse 3 *For consider him that endured such contradiction of sinners against himself, lest ye be wearied and faint in your minds.* (To faint in your mind would be like passing out and unable to do anything.)

Verse 4 *Ye have not yet resisted unto blood, striving against sin.* (We have not been called upon to shed our blood this way.)

Verses 5-7 *⁵And ye have forgotten the exhortation which speaketh unto you as unto children, My son, despise not thou the chastening of the Lord, nor faint when thou art rebuked of him: ⁶For whom the Lord loveth he chasteneth, and scourgeth every son whom he receiveth ⁷If ye endure chastening, God dealeth with you as with sons; for what son is he whom the father chasteneth not? ⁸But if ye be without chastisement, whereof all are partakers, then are ye bastards, and not sons.* (So many have taught chastisement is sickness and diseases then that would mean all who become Christians are to be made sick, and that really goes against the rewards and blessings that come with righteousness.)

The Lord, like any good Father, will chastise you when you refuse to hear: Job 33:14-17 *17For God speaketh once, yea twice, yet man perceiveth it not.*

15In a dream, in a vision of the night, when deep sleep falleth upon men, in slumberings upon the bed; 16Then he openeth the ears of men, and sealeth their instruction, 17That he may withdraw man from his purpose, and hide pride from man. The Lord will chastise us when we commit sins and iniquities.

2 Samuel 7:14 *I will be his father, and he shall be my son. If he commit iniquity, I will chasten him with the rod of men, and with the stripes of the children of men:*

He will also chastise when you provoke Him, like King David did. Sounds like King David may have suffered with some grievous disease after sinning with Bathsheba for a while as you study this.

Psalm 6:14 *I will be his father, and he shall be my son. If he commit iniquity, I will chasten him with the rod of men, and with the stripes of the children of men:*

1 Corinthians 11:31-32 *31For if we would judge ourselves, we should not be judged. 32But when we are judged, we are chastened of the Lord, that we should not be condemned with the world.*

The Lord tell us in Galatians 6:7-8 *7Be not deceived; God is not mocked: for whatsoever a man soweth, that shall he also reap 8For he that soweth to his flesh shall of the flesh reap corruption; but he that soweth to the Spirit shall of the Spirit reap life everlasting.*

Applying the Word of Truth

We have hopefully effectively exposed the spirit of self-pity that has infiltrated many of God's people in the churches today. We have learned we really need to rid ourselves of it in the name of Jesus. It is time to stop dragging about all these unclean things that weight you down.

Hebrews 12:1 *Wherefore seeing we also are compassed about with so great a cloud of witnesses, let us lay aside every weight, and the sin which doth so easily beset us, and let us run with patience the race that is set before us.*

Self-pity is a sin because it is fear based and does not require any faith. Whatsoever is not of faith is sin, including some of the foods people fear and then eat anyway. I know I should not eat that decadent cake or pie, it's not good for me, but then I do it anyway.

Romans 14:23 *And he that doubteth is damned if he eat, because [he eateth] not of faith: for whatsoever [is] not of faith is sin.*

The Bible tells us in 1 John 5:15-17 *¹⁵And if we know that he hear us, whatsoever we ask, we know that we have the petitions that we desired of him. ¹⁶If any man see his brother sin a sin which is not unto death, he shall ask, and he shall give him life for them that sin not unto death. There is a sin unto death: I do not say that he shall pray for it. ¹⁷All unrighteousness is sin: and there is a sin not unto death.*

I would say that a "sin unto death" would be a sin that produces a "disease unto death." John is saying here do not even pray for that person until you are able to minister first, so they recognize and repent of those things, otherwise, their prayers may not be answered. For the same reason the Lord taught people preaching the Gospel to cast out evil spirits before healing the people. Forgiveness is the main key to enter into God's presence and Holiness.

So, if you have really forgiven from your heart then you don't have to keep telling that old story over and over again about what someone did to you and why you can't let it go. You can recognize that it is not your thoughts, but a spirit of self-pity trying to keep you in an unholy agreement or covenant so God cannot bless you.

When you keep holding on to a record of wrongs against yourself or someone, no matter how evil it was, you are giving a place for the devil in your life and in your body. That is always supported by the spirit of bitterness, which comes in first. That works the same way against other nations and wars fought. Jesus commanded us to love everyone including our enemies.

Matthew 5:10-12 *¹⁰Blessed are they which are persecuted for righteousness' sake: for theirs is the kingdom of heaven. ¹¹Blessed are ye, when men shall revile you, and persecute you, and shall say all manner of evil against you falsely, for my sake. ¹²Rejoice, and be exceeding glad: for great is your reward in heaven: for so persecuted they the prophets which were before you.*

A spirit of bitterness, if left unchecked, can eat away at you like a cancer. It is very dangerous and we have seen that is one of the main roots in most cancer cases.

We are to obey the Lord and forgive all who offended us and then resist the devil, which is every evil spirit of the devil's kingdom like self-pity, and he will flee from you.

James 4:7 *Submit yourselves therefore to God. Resist the devil, and he will flee from you.*

You must simply trust Papa God will deal with those who have done you and others wrong. First off, we must always remember that it is not really the person, but the evil spirit, that is being allowed to manifest its fallen nature through the person, from lack of their knowledge, because they have believed the devils lies instead of the Gospel truth.

Who's Battle is it Anyway?

Let us not behave as the world would behave, running out into a battle with our swords drawn or guns blazing. With a reckless anger and attitude that if we suffer a few causalities here and there that is just the nature of war. That is where they get the saying, "Fools rush in where Angels fear to dread."

No, God's way is always patient, it is not antagonistic, or offensive. It is putting on the sacrifice of praise. For the battle is not yours, but God's.

2 Chronicles 20:15 *And he said, Hearken ye, all Judah, and ye inhabitants of Jerusalem, and thou king Jehoshaphat, Thus saith the LORD unto you, Be not afraid nor dismayed by reason of this great multitude; for the battle is not yours, but God's.*

You might be feeling tired and weary, but our Lord is always strong and never gets tired. You might feel like the situation is hopeless and you feel a bit helpless. But God is the Lord of miracles and He is our Hope for everything hopeless and He is our help when we feel helpless. If a spirit of doubt and unbelief tries to discourage you, just remember the Cross of Jesus.

The Apostle Paul says in Roman 8:31 *What shall we then say to these things? If God be for us, who can be against us?*

Think about this it goes on to say in verse 32: *He that spared not his own Son, but delivered him up for us all, how shall he not with him also freely give us all things?*

There it is! When I consider the cross, all I can see is God's amazing love. I see how Papa God gave up His only begotten Son into the cruelest of death, once and forever, eliminating our greatest problem in life, the problem of our sin that separates us from a Holy God.

And if Papa God would do that for you, if He would make that kind of sacrifice just for you, then how could we not trust Him completely and have faith that He can surely be trusted to fight our battles with us and for us?

When that happens it will be a very fearful thing for those who have sinned against us to fall into the hands of God.

1 Chronicles 16:22 *Saying, Touch not mine anointed, and do my prophets no harm..*

Hebrews 10:31 *It is a fearful thing to fall into the hands of the living God.*

It will be much worse for them then anything you could have ever thought to do or say to them, because the battle belongs to the Lord. God will deal with them in His perfect timing. Don't forget Romans 12:20 *Therefore if thine enemy hunger, feed him; if he thirst, give him drink: for in so doing thou shalt heap coals of fire on his head.*

And in Matthew 10:28 it says: *And fear not them which kill the body, but are not able to kill the soul: but rather fear him which is able to destroy both soul and body in hell.*

Also in Acts 7:59 it says: *And they stoned Stephen, calling upon God, and saying, Lord Jesus, receive my spirit. 60And he kneeled down, and cried with a loud voice, Lord, lay not this sin to their charge. And when he had said this, he fell asleep.*

And then in Luke 23:34 *Jesus said, Father forgive them for they know not what they do.*

What do you think we should be doing? How much more do we need to forgive everyone and ourselves?

God may deal with those who have offended and wronged you now, or He may deal with them later in the next life, either way no one made you their judge on earth.

However, we can be aware of people's fruit, whether it's good or bad, and use that discernment to continue in friendship, or withdraw from that individual.

2 Thessalonians 3:6 *Now we command you, brethren, in the name of our Lord Jesus Christ, that ye withdraw yourselves from every brother that walketh disorderly, and not after the tradition which he received of us.*

Galatians 6:1 *Brethren, if a man be overtaken in a fault, ye which are spiritual, restore such an one in the spirit of meekness; considering thyself, lest thou also be tempted.*

Again, be sure you are speaking to an individual from the Holy Ghost, not out of your own will or desire. Because you just might fall yourself.

Conclusion

How amazing is it that the Lord of all creation would adopt us into His Holy family and then allow us to partner with Him through Jesus Christ of Nazareth that this and greater things shall we do according to John 14:12 *Verily, verily, I say unto you, He that believeth on me, the works that I do shall he do also; and greater works than these shall he do; because I go unto my Father.*

So it seems to me that Papa God's part is to perform miracles, heal, restore, and to provide for us; our part is to be readily available for Him to use as we stay in faith and trust Him always for everything.

I am just going to believe the Lord and ask that He release the Holy Ghost now on everyone who is reading this. That the Holy Ghost will show you and direct you here.

We are going to take the time to recognize the issues in our life. We are going to take responsibility for all of them and repent and change the way we think about it forever Amen. We are going to think about it the way our Lord thinks about it. There is no disease or poverty in Heaven. We are to bring some of Heaven to earth today.

We are going to humble ourselves before the invisible, immortal, mighty hand of our Lord that He may exalt us in due time. Today let us remove those things that are hindering us and remove the things that would prevent us from being blessed. As you know we can cast these unclean spirits out and it seems a good idea to do it often in case some others tried to come in their place.

If you have taken communion in the past, and most likely everyone reading this has done that unworthily, if you were in ignorance and lacking knowledge about it, let us first repent of that.

Pray the following out loud from your heart:

Papa God my Lord and Savior, forgive me for partaking of the bread and drinking of the Lord's cup when I was filled with unforgiveness and any other unclean spirits towards others, myself or you. I know now that it is not the sacraments that save me, it is my obedience.

Forgive me for entertaining a spirit of fear in my life, which brought stress and anxiety. For that spirit of fear of failing others; for fear of man which put me into performance and perfectionism. That caused me to have an inability to receive love without that stinking spirit of fear attached. I repent for all projected fear and projected rejection; that projection that caused me to think my earthly father or someone in a powerful position over me would reject me. I know now that was a lie from the pit of Hell, because you Lord did not reject me.

Please help me to stop right now rejecting myself. I repent for entertaining that stinking foul unloving spirit; for that spirit of self destructive behaviors; for all the self indulgences and spirit of self-pity; for all the addictive spirits and spirits of rebellion and insecurity; for double-mindedness and for all perverted spirits that caused me to lust in my flesh instead of give love in my spirit. I also repent for entertaining the spirit of death right now in the all powerful name of Jesus Christ of Nazareth, Amen.

Now I will pray in agreement with you:

Right now by the authority I have been given in Jesus Christ of Nazareth's name, I cast out every spirit named just now by my brothers and sisters reading this and I command that the stinking, foul, unclean evil spirits go at once to the dry place. You have to obey me now, Go! I ask Papa God that you do a creative miracle where needed here and bring my brothers and sisters back into homeostasis and help them maintain it. That you put back those things and parts the devil messed with and tried to destroy, the way that they are supposed to be before the foundation of the world was laid.

That spirits like Type I and II Diabetes and cancer can no longer come against these precious children of Christ. Every spirit of type 1 and II diabetes I break your power and command you go at once to the dry place. Every unclean spirit of infirmity and disease go now, we know who you are and we have power over you according to our Lord so you must go now. Every spirit of cancer and spirits of bitterness, I break your power and command you to go now with diabetes and spirits of infirmity and diseases and every other foul anti-Christ spirits.

I command that all your chemistry balances out now and that your body begins at once to repair

itself of any damage and that you be made whole
and well and prosper. I ask this Papa God in the all
powerful name of your son Jesus Christ of Nazareth. Amen.

Chapter 6

Self-Pity and Relationships

Without proper communication, every relationship will somehow suffer, including our relationship with the Lord. While we have been exposing the spirit of self-pity one thing is apparent, there is often an unclean unloving spirit that tries to altar what is actually being communicated so a misunderstanding will occur. When that happens, someone is offended and the devil is de-lighted.

One of the things most people engage in everyday is communicating on some level, and it really can be quite complicated at times, just trying to get someone to understand, I mean look how hard it is as a believer to just get someone to understand that you really care about them, or how much Jesus really loves them and took their place on that cross so you wouldn't ever have to. Or trying to get someone to understand there is an invisible spiritual world at work in our everyday natural world, and to learn to discern what is manifesting in others and yourself.

Again I just feel lead to remind you that a spirit of self-pity is not just a human emotion, nor is it a psychological defect. Even if you grew up in a household of generational professional self-pity-ist, there is hope for you, because if you learn the truth, it will make you free.

John 8:31-32 *31Then said Jesus to those Jews which believed on him, If ye continue in my word, then are ye my disciples indeed; 32And ye shall know the truth, and the truth shall make you free.*

A spirit of fear, which we now call stress and anxiety, will apparently launch an attack in your thought life, projecting vain imaginations that try to exalt them-selves against the knowledge of God. If you make any agreement with it, you are helping establish the kingdom of hell on earth rather then bringing some Heaven to earth.

I think it really comes down to replacing old thinking patterns learned in the past with how we think about everything now as a Believer.

1 Corinthians 10:31 *Whether therefore ye eat, or drink, or whatsoever ye do, do all to the glory of God.*

One of the reasons it is so vital to study God's instructions to us, is that it enables us to be more sensitive to the leading of the Holy Spirit, Who consequently is able to help navigate us through this life from a heavenly perspective. This Spirit enables us with the truth to help us to not get ensnared and tricked by the lusts and sinful ways of this fallen world.

The Great Illusionist

This is the day God has made; the devil did not make this day. The devil is like an illusionist; as he is distracting you with one hand, he is hiding something or performs a trick with the other hand. The devil is great at deceiving that is what he does. He continually lies and deceives you trying to pull you into some place of sin to kill, steal, and destroy you.

Most people who fall into sin will do it when they think no one else can see them sinning. Only God sees everything. There is nothing you can hide from Him.

The devil, in a way, has worked his deceptions and illusions into a form of science. Because he understands how the human eye sees certain elements, he wants to deceive our eyes into seeing something that is not true. Everything in Occultism is hiding some truth by deception. Just like as in a total eclipse of the sun. The sun is still there, but something is in front of your perception, hiding it from you.

For example, when the devil brings a symptom, he

is hoping you will entertain the spirit of fear that accompanies it so it can soon become a real sickness and disease.

Remember: the devil can even appear as an angel of light; it's one of his best tricks, and he is very adept at using a full range of his spiritual dramatic stage effects with all the lying signs and wonders, with smoke and lights and mirrors. Lest anyone forget, he has extensive knowledge of the Bible and about how the human mind operates.

The devil wants to lead people away from God and the Gospel truth so they are ignorant of spiritual things.

He will even use things like film and entertainment to sow seeds of compromise into your life. All you need to do is consider Hollywood, and the things you watch, has it brought you closer or further from God?

The enemy will use well-educated people who do not realize God calls them a fool whenever he can to destroy morality. A spirit of doubt and unbelief has blinded them to everything, which cannot be seen with the bodily eyes.

Psalm 14:1 *The fool hath said in his heart, there is no God.*

They do not realize that God sees and records in Heaven everything they do and they will give an account one day for how they lived their life and how the devil used them to lead others astray. We are fighting an invisible battle everyday that starts in our thought lives.

What You Can't See Can Hurt You

Bacteria, which is invisible to the naked eye, was first observed by Antonie van Leeuwenhoek in 1676, using a single-lens microscope that he designed.

He actually called them "animalcules" when he published his observations in a series of letters to the Royal Society of Science.

Do you think the general public may have thought this was foolish rubbish thinking, that there were invisible things like Bacteria around causing sickness and diesease? Then around 1859, Louis Pasteur came along and was able to demonstrate there really was something to this invisible germ business. At this point it was still considered the germ theory of disease. The medical world had deplorable practices back then by today's standards. One of the most unhealthy germ infested places you could contract a disease was in hospitals. Doctors would handle dealing with a corps and then go deliver a baby without first washing their hands and wonder why the baby and mother would end up getting sick and die.

From his personal observations, a doctor named Ignaz Semmelweis figured out that hand-washing drastically reduced the mortality rate of delivering babies to below 1%. As a result, he was in terrible conflict with the established scientific and medical opinions of the times. His outrageous ideas of washing your hands were offensive and rejected by the medical community of his day. As he could offer no acceptable scientific explanation for his findings, this doctor ended up losing his practice and medical licensing, and was committed to an asylum, where he died at age 48 of septicemia, a serious infection of the blood.

His idea finally earned widespread acceptance years after his death, when Louis Pasteur confirmed the germ theory was more then a mere theory, but was indeed a fact.

How many people in the churches are offended that we dare teach about invisible evil spirits and cast them out in Jesus' name? Or that we believe God said what He means and means what He said. I heard a popular radio and television preacher the other day talk about salvation and did not hear him say much at all about repenting of your sins and continuing to pursue a sanctified life. It is not popular to suggest or talk about evil spirits; however the Lord Jesus did teach about it whenever He had a church service.

Nowhere in the Bible have I found where it says to just ask Jesus into your hearts. It says repent and be baptized, to be saved in His name.

Matthew 4:17 *From that time Jesus began to preach, and to say, Repent, for the kingdom of heaven is at hand.*

In the second chapter of Acts, the Lord used Peter to bring conviction on the people, who probably contributed to having killed the only begotten Son of God. In verse 37 they cry out, "What shall we do?" In Acts 2:38 "Then Peter said unto them, repent and be baptized everyone of you in the name of Jesus Christ for the remission of your sins." Peter never said to ask Jesus into your hearts.

As a pastor, I am greatly concerned when I hear someone share a faulty watered-down Gospel message that you can be saved and continue living a worldly existence because somehow Grace covers you. What will become of those who teach and have been taught such doctrines of devils when they cry out Lord, Lord and Jesus turns and says to them, "I never knew you depart from me, ye that work iniquity" (Matthew 7:23).

Jesus even said in Matthew 18:6 *But whoso shall offend one of these little ones which believe in me, it were better for him that a millstone were hanged about his neck, and that he were drowned in the depth of the sea.*

Believe and Teach What the Holy Bible Says

The devil and his demons will try to encourage sin in every place they can to separate you from the truth of the Gospel and His love... So the world is filled with heresies and deceitful ways now to promote schism and offenses in the churches. I mean, many people seem to get really upset and bent out of shape if your beliefs differ from what they've been taught and believe.

Just try talking about things like the return of Christ, so many people have opinions based on lack of knowledge that topics like this could turn into a debate. They have opinions without even studying the Bible, without being *Berean* to make sure that is really what the Lord said.

Matthew 24:24 *For there shall arise false Christs, and false prophets, and shall shew great signs and wonders; insomuch that, if it were possible, they shall deceive the very elect.*

2 Corinthians 11:13-15 *[13]For such are false apostles, deceitful workers, transforming themselves into the apostles of Christ. [14]And no marvel; for Satan himself is transformed into an angel of light. [15]Therefore it is no great thing if his ministers also be transformed as the ministers of righteousness; whose end shall be according to their works.*

The Lord had the apostle Peter give us a prophesy that in the last days scoffers and skeptics would be arguing against the possibility of Christ's return.

2 Peter 3:3-4 *[3]Knowing this first, that there shall come in the last days scoffers, walking after their own lusts, [4]And saying, Where is the promise of his coming? for since the fathers fell asleep, all things continue as they were from the beginning of the creation.*

No, things have not just continued as they were, things are being set up as never before in all of history, and many prophecies have now taken place since Israel became a nation again after being scattered for so many years.

And as soon as they divide Jerusalem up, the rest of

the major prophecies will take place. The Bible tells us to rejoice again and again.

But one of the best tricks the devil has, is leading someone into despair and opening them up to receive the spirit of self-pity.

Agreeing with a doctrine of devils would have someone clinging to this world and afraid of the Rapture, as a spirit of fear projects into your future and the unknown. Studying the Bible reveals those places you think are unknown, and brings you into His peace because the Lord reveals it to us.

John 15:15 *Henceforth I call you not servants; for the servant knoweth not what his lord doeth: but I have called you friends; for all things that I have heard of my Father I have made known unto you.*

Mark 13:23 *But take ye heed: behold, I have foretold you all things.*

Proverbs 25:2 *It is the glory of God to conceal a thing: but the honour of kings is to search out a matter.*

As we study the Word of God, we will find peace and healing.

No matter what you do, what sort of job you might have, from taking care of children, managing an office, flying an airplane to a doctor performing surgery, every butcher, to baker, to candle stick maker in this world, has to deal with the enemy of our souls doing all he can to try and get us stressed out. Still a modern word for a spirit of fear that God did not give you (2 Timothy 1:7)

Again the Bible tells us... for whatsoever is not of faith is sin... Romans 14:23

Romans 12:2 *And be not conformed to this world: but be ye transformed by the renewing of your mind, that ye may prove what is that good, and acceptable, and perfect, will of God.*

I just want to encourage you to simply practice taking inventory of your thought life on a regular basis. Make sure your thoughts are pleasing to God and they line up with being obedient to Christ. If we were not able to bring into captivity every thought to the obedience of Christ, the Lord would not have told us we could.

2 Corinthians 10:5 *Casting down imaginations, and every high thing that exalteth itself against the knowledge of God, and bringing into captivity every thought to the obedience of Christ;*

Just as you learn to practice an instrument or a sport, any thing that takes some skill, the more you practice the easier it will become.

Why does the Lord tell us to renew our minds? Because it helps continue to transform us into being saints instead of sinners.

In fact, modern scientific research is now showing that in as little as 4 days, if you persists and keep practicing, thinking about things in a godly way, staying in faith and resisting the spirit of fear, you will begin to dismantle those thorny toxic branches of thoughts that have built up strong holds in your minds by the enemy of your soul. In as little as 4 days time, you can start growing healthy branches of thoughts if you stay consistent.

It will take about 21 days to actually establish a new memory without the toxic thorns. As you replace those old toxic thoughts, you grow new healthy ones, establishing healthy memories from Godly thinking over the old toxic ones the devil helped establish there.

All the more reason to have some Scriptures you can meditate on—bringing healing to all your flesh. So when you find a toxic thought, trying to respond to any situation in your life, you can replace it with God's Holy Word instead.

As You Get in the Word the Word Gets into You

Why do you think the Lord tells us in Matthew 12:36 *But I say unto you, That every idle word that men shall speak, they shall give account thereof in the day of judgment.*

All words, even idle ones, have power in them, and there is no such thing as empty words. Each word counts for something. When any word makes a sound and leaves your mouth it first evolved as a thought.

There are probably countless switches and neurons firing across the synapse in your brain, things in your body going off and on in you and in your soul, and spirit, before the action of a word finally comes forward.

The Lord tells us to get wisdom, so we do not perish from lack of knowledge.

In this fallen world, there will be troubles, and we are called to be more than conquerors; we are called to be overcomers, that through Christ who strengthens us we can overcome all things. The Lord Jesus tell us in John 16:33 *These things I have spoken unto you, that in me ye might have peace. In the world ye shall have tribulation: but be of good cheer; I have overcome the world.*

Again we read in Psalm 34:19 *Many are the afflictions of the righteous: but the LORD delivereth him out of them all.*

Maybe it's time we quit being impressed with the problems and symptoms the enemy tries to bring to us, and focus on what God has to say about it instead. After all, out of the abundance of the heart, your mouth speaks. So the question is, what are you full of? You can tell by what falls out of your mouth, and you will reap blessings or afflictions. Always remember: proclaiming what God has said always brings blessings.

Luke 6:45 *A good man out of the good treasure of his heart bringeth forth that which is good; and an evil man out of the evil treasure of his heart bringeth forth that which is evil: for of the abundance of the heart his mouth speaketh.*

This world has always been a dangerous place since the fall of Adam. However, instead of getting safer in many ways, we seem worse off in these modern times. As now we have the ability to not just kill with swords, but to blow up the entire earth!

The people and ministers in the Bible did not have cell phones and pagers going off day and night which can try and bring someone into drivenness and perfectionism.

In a way, the world today, with such modern advances in technology, has brought in tremendous amounts of spirits of fear, anxiety, and stress. So now there is a continual bombardment on your senses, even just driving down a rode and seeing billboards can assault your senses. The pornography industry has even found ways to come through cell phones recently, besides televisions and the computers.

2 Timothy 3:1-5 *¹This know also, that in the last days perilous times shall come. ²For men shall be lovers of their own selves, covetous, boasters, proud, blasphemers, disobedient to parents, unthankful, unholy, ³Without natural affection, trucebreakers, false accusers, incontinent, fierce, despisers of those that are good, ⁴Traitors, heady, highminded, lovers of pleasures more than lovers of God; ⁵Having a form of godliness, but denying the power thereof: from such turn away.*

Gone are the simple ways of family life from our society today. Even children are becoming specialists about certain subject matters, and seem to have a spirit of resentment against their parents for being so ignorant of such things. They are being taught by the enemy, through the media, to be "disobedient to their parents."

Age of Technology

The devil, along with the spirit of self–pity, has taught people to live a self-centered existence. We really live in a fallen selfish world but still good can overcome the bad. As believers, we are not to live the way the world does.

The Lord warned through prophecy, that before His return, there will be advances in knowledge. And we see today, with the use of technology and internet, that has been fulfilled.

Daniel 12:4 *But thou, O Daniel, shut up the words, and seal the book, even to the time of the end: many shall run to and fro, and knowledge shall be increased.*

From my personal observations with all the complicated gadgets we have today, it seems we have much less time to communicate with our families and friends. As new technologies appear to makes communication so much easier, we also seem to be much more distant and fragmented in our relationships.

Since the invention of personal computers, anyone can access instant communication everywhere in this world. However, with all the new technology we are facing new problems. Our society seems to be falling apart and becoming morally corrupted, depleted and bankrupted of Godly ways. And all along the church today wants to give a popular message about Grace on steroids, so you do not have to take any personal responsibility to repent and turn from sin.

Even if people are living longer, they are not really healthier, and they are certainly not happier. This can bring in a spirit of quiet desperation and self-pity. Along with wars and rumors of war, each day seems to have its fill of chaos and crisis all around us. Maybe truthfully much of the chaos and crisis is something we are contributing to, unaware of our selfish ways wanting to control our world.

In the last days it says in 2 Timothy 3:1-2 *¹This know also, that in the last days perilous times shall come. ²For men shall be lovers of their own selves.*

Our Brains are Marvelously Made

No one can control your thought life without your permission. No evil spirit is going to manifest once you recognize how it has been using you to express itself. By taking our thoughts captive to the obedience of Christ, we can proclaim and confess the promise of God and walk in blessings instead of curses.

How many times have you heard yourself complain to someone that you're having a bad day? It was not a coincidence if you woke up feeling negative and then as you continue throughout your day, things happen and help fuel the release of more toxic negative chemicals, pretty much affecting everything you say and do? This is one of the things a spirit of self-pity is trying to do, and so you lose your joy and peace.

If you don't learn to control your thought life in Christ, that sort of thing will color your world, so everything seems to look rather bleak.

That is how a spirit of self-pity wants to manifest in you.

You must understand and remember that thoughts are very real physical things triggering switches inside your brain, and are changing moment-by-moment as you are thinking.

Again this is what science is now calling neuroplasticity or brain malleability. God designed our brains with the amazing ability to reorganize itself throughout our lifetime here on earth. Neuroplasticity allows the neurons or the (nerve cells) in your brain to compensate for any problems they are dealing with. For example, your brain is wired to make adjustments for any diseases or injury, even from accidents. It will adjust itself to the changes and any activities in response to any new situations or to any changes in environment. The Lord created us with so many wonderful things. We are renewing our minds to God's Holy Word—a process that takes place to rid ourselves of toxic thoughts.

It really is quite astounding how the Lord created us to be so fearful and wonderfully made, and we should be praising Him in this as we are told in:

Psalm 139:14 *I will praise thee; for I am fearfully and wonderfully made: marvellous are thy works; and that my soul knoweth right well.*

Our brain has this marvelous way of reorganization that takes place by mechanisms such as something called "axonal sprouting." This occurs when, in an injury, any undamaged axons grow new nerve endings to reconnect neurons where they need to be connected. Those undamaged axons can also sprout nerve endings and connect with other undamaged nerve cells, by coming together and forming new neural pathways to accomplish whatever function is needed.

For example, if you were unfortunately injured in an accident, and one hemisphere of your brain was damaged, the hemisphere of your brain that was unharmed, may take over some of its functions of the damaged side, as part of the healing process begins. So your amazingly complex brain is designed by the Lord to compensate for the damage that was done in effect by reorganizing itself and forming new connections between the neurons that are intact. It does seem the neurons need to be stimulated through activity in order to reconnect.

Now again whatever the devil does, whatever he tries to destroy, God can recreate in a miracle and put it back the way He designed it to be.

The devil understands Neuroplasticity, and at times if he is able he will try and use it for harm by contributing to some kind of impairment. For example, he will assign a deaf and dumb spirit to cause someone to suffer from deafness, but then he will cause a continual ringing in their ears which the doctor will diagnose as tinnitus, which can result from the rewiring of brain cells starving for some sounds. Renewing your minds to God's Word would certainly be advisable for those neurons to form beneficial connections; they must be correctly stimulated which is what mediating on the Word of God will do.

I'll tell you the truth, when you allow yourself to entertain a negative toxic thought; you are in fact releasing the wrong chemicals into your body. That negative thought passing though your brain is actually causing a dangerous toxic impact.

That spirit of criticism and heaviness will cause you a problem if you allow it to continue.

Proverbs 25:28 *He that hath no rule over his own spirit is like a city that is broken down, and without walls.*

So any animal or creature can come and go as it pleases and leave any mess it likes. When you entertain those negative and critical toxic thoughts, it is not going to just stay in one place in your mind, it will not stay isolated to one area in your brain. It's going to have a dangerous impact like leaving a fox loose in the hen house. That loose toxic negative thought is going to end up colouring a vast majority of your active thoughts; it will have an impact on your perceptions and your attitude. Until, of course, you decide you have had enough, and turn back to the Lord for help. It's up to you to stay in agreement with the spirit of self-pity which will keep you floating about in a sea of unforgiveness, or follow what the Lord says and forgive from your hearts.

Those evil spirits want to keep feeding you toxic negative thoughts because it spreads in you like a virus through your mind and will affect your whole being.

The place where neurons (your thoughts) are collected and stored only really takes up about 15% of your brain cells, the rest appear to be made up of glial cells.

Glial cells are those cells that interact with the neurons, and help control them to work properly. They seem to have all sorts of functions to help with communications between thoughts. They are designed to help prune off toxic thoughts as well as send signals between thought networks so they are sending information to help activate and speedily help with cognitive processing and building memories.

So the attitude that one thought brings will then quickly impact a sequence of thoughts and affect their attitudes, like knocking down rows of dominoes.

The more you are aware of your thought life and how it is working, the easier it becomes to deal with it. You really have to take charge here and not allow just any thought to wander about your mind. Demand to see its passport and when in doubt cast it out!

Just the way you are able to discipline yourself to learn to do any task by disciplining your thoughts, you must take each thought captive to the obedience of Christ, to stop the spread of the devil's lies and evil spirits from freely wandering through your minds. Then they can no longer manifest their evil nature in us. Papa God designed us to live forever, and wants us to succeed and prosper through the Lord Jesus Christ of Nazareth.

Discerning the Spirit of Self-Pity

So we need to discern and recognize that vile spirit of self-pity as our enemy and call it a sin because it is so dangerous to our health and well being.

People who come from certain denominational backgrounds have challenged me and will ask if God always heals?

Can you find any place in all the Holy Bible where God refused to heal someone who came to Him with a humble heart?

1 John 1:5 *This then is the message which we have heard of him, and declare unto you, that God is light, and in him is no darkness at all.*

In Him there is no darkness at all, when you turn on a light darkness disappears!

I ask you, can darkness come out of light any more than sickness and disease can come out of health?

If you are in any agreement with a spirit of self-pity, and you do well to recognize it now, just take responsibility and repent before Papa God in Jesus Christ of Nazareth's name.

Hebrews 13: 17 *Obey them that have the rule over you, and submit yourselves: for they watch for your souls, as they that must give account, that they may do it with joy, and not with grief: for that is unprofitable for you.*

I would say that anyone who is not capable of guiding you safely into heaven, would be just like the captain of a ship that sinks to the bottom of the ocean—unfit to be a leader in the church, no matter how popular they might be. As a Pastor I am going to be held accountable for how I tended to God's flock. Every Pastor will some day stand before the eternal living Lord Jesus and give an account of not only what we did, but what his flock did or didn't do for the Lord. So I take this position very seriously. I pray you recognize that God has appointed your Pastor, and that is where his authority comes from "them that have the rule over you..."

James 3:1 *My brethren, be not many masters, knowing that we shall receive the greater condemnation.*

That word "masters," is referring to teachers of God's Word.

Hebrews 13: 18-21 *¹⁸Pray for us: for we trust we have a good conscience, in all things willing to live honestly. ¹⁹But I beseech you the rather to do this, that I may be restored to you the sooner. ²⁰Now the God of peace, that brought again from the dead our Lord Jesus, that great shepherd of the sheep, through the blood of the everlasting covenant, ²¹Make you perfect in every good work to do his will, working in you that which is wellpleasing in his sight, through Jesus Christ; to whom be glory for ever and ever. Amen.*

If today's church would simply meet Papa God's conditions as the 120 did on the day of Pentecost, how could we not experience the same sort of results? How odd is it that over five hundred people saw the resurrected Jesus Christ of Nazareth at the same time and only 120 of them did as He instructed?

1 Corinthians 15:6 *After that, he was seen of above five hundred brethren at once; of whom the greater part remain unto this present, but some are fallen asleep.*

The power the Lord gave to the apostles, and then the 70 has never disappeared from the true believers. Sadly the churches did not heed the warning in 2 Timothy 3:5 *and turn away from those who had a form of godliness but denied the power thereof;* it's time to recover our unlimited faith and believe again, so the Lord will confirm His Word with mighty signs and wonders following.

Exhortation

May the Lord now release you to fulfill the very purpose of God in your life that He's called you to, and prepared you for, and ordained you, before the foundations of the world was formed. May you fulfill all the desires that God has for you, that cause you now to truly thirst and hunger for the Word of God and His righteousness in all you do. That you are also fulfilled by His righteousness and drink and eat of His living water and spiritual food that you will never hunger and thirst again.

That you are able to always sense His presence, and that His Holy Spirit lead you always.

And may you not be fearful of anything or ever intimidated or threatened by anything.

So that you are in control of your thoughts and that you take your thoughts captive to the obedience of Christ.

That you are a blessed person and that the blessings of the Lord chase you down and overtake you always.

That you shall rise up and see your life come into its full destiny, in the name of the Lord.

Some of you feel like your best years are now behind you but the Lord is saying your best years are still ahead.

In fact, the very things you feel were mistakes in your life, or that you have deeply regretted, the Lord will now work out for good.

Romans 8:28 *And we know that all things work together for good to them that love God, to them who are the called according to his purpose.*

Those times that you cursed others or yourself; when you heard those negative things spewing out of your own mouth, the Lord is able to turn it around and cause blessings to come from it.

The Lord is giving you a taste of who He is.

That you even now in a real tangible way say, "O taste and see the goodness of the Lord."

As the Holy Spirit causes living waters to flow out of you it is washing you clean and causing you to be changed right now within your heart.

The Lord God loves you and is changing things and orchestrating things to bless your life right now. From within your heart, you're going to know the goodness and blessings of the Lord for your life as supernatural blessings overtake you as you are obedient to His commandments

That you are filled with Christ's love and continue in His Word.

Those things the enemy has done in your life are going to be turned around and good will come of it, things are going to change quickly for you, to bless you, as you let the Word of God change your heart and change your tongue.

Conditions to Healing

If you want to experience the pleasures of God, you will need to make Jesus the Lord over all your life in everything you do in every breath you take in every thought you examine and think through in obedience to His Holy Word.

As you meditate on His Word day and night, it brings healing and health and blessings and causes you to prosper as your soul prospers.

With your mouth, proclaim the Gospel. With your mouth ask for the forgiveness of your sins and iniquities because of Christ shed blood, and begin to use your tongue to bless others. As you forgive from your heart, you erase the record of wrongs done. And as you do that, I tell you the truth, you are going to experience God's Holy pleasure.

You're going to be like that runner in Chariots of Fire film and you will feel the glory of the Lord as you run this race.

Closing Prayer

Papa God, what a wonderful Father You are. We want to thank You for shedding light on this evil spirit of self-pity, so that we can get free from the enemy. As we continue in your Word and in Your Truth, and receive Your Love, we are given discernment to cast out all unclean spirits, thoughts, and dis-ease from our lives. Thank you for providing us the means to take back our lives to the Glory of You, Lord. Continue working with us as you expose self-pity in every area of our lives. We want to be completely free so that we can experience ALL You have for us. In Jesus Christ of Nazareth's precious name, Amen.

About the Author

Caspar McCloud was born in Ohio, and later moved to the UK. He legally changed his name as a teenager as countless entertainers and performers have done before him. As he pursued a career as a professional musician and recording artist, he is now known as an outstanding virtuoso guitarist, singer, and songwriter, an accomplished portrait artist, as well as an equestrian, ordained minister, and author. He signed to Atlantic Records after leaving his home in England for New York City and was touted as the next Jimi Hendrix by Ahmet Ertegun, the CEO of Atlantic Records. As an accomplished musician, he has completed several projects over the years, since his first UK release, " Messin Round," Caspar McCloud and the Ministry of Three produced, *In Adoration, The Living Word, Soul Saved*, and, *In Our Life Time*. There are also several solo projects like "*Mercy, Grace and Love*" that features more of his classical/celtic/worship acoustic style. He has played and or recorded with many celebrities and friends including, Michael Shrieve, and Michael Carabella of Santana, Matt Bassionett, of Joe Satriani band-G3 and Ringo Starr band, Eddie Zynn of FogHat, and Hall and Oats, Phil Keaggy, Peter Furler and Jody Davis of the Newsboys, to name a few.

Caspar is also a world-class portrait artist with a pre-Raphaelite approach, specializing in equestrian subject matter, and he has some of his work in the personal collections of English royalty.

Along with all these activities, he is also a husband and father of two children.

Caspar's first book was his incredible autobiography entitled, *Nothing is Impossible*, which portrays signs and wonders and miracles.

He presently pastors a church called, "The Upper Room," in Canton, GA, when he is not out traveling as a musician and a guest speaker. To contact Caspar McCloud for more information on his book, music, art, and ministry, go to www.pastorcaspar.com or email to pastorcaspar@gmail.com or on facebook: Caspar Mc-Cloud Ministries.

What Others Have Said About Caspar

"Caspar McCloud is the next Jimi Hendrix" —Ahmet Ertegun, President, Atlantic Records

"Why, he is a modern-day renaissance man!" —The 700 Club

"Caspar McCloud floats in the clouds—heavenly music, spiritual inspiration, a gentle spirit in touch with his God." —Robert Lacey, Best-selling Author, London England

"Caspar McCloud is a multi-talented artist. He not only makes music with a guitar but with a paint brush as well. His love of horses is evident in his highly rendered and exquisite equestrian paintings that capture every nuance. Caspar inspires people on many levels." —Bart Lindstrom, Artist Portrait Society of America

"What is there left to say about the musical genius that is Caspar McCloud? Not only is the man a true gentleman, but he is a gifted painter (as in, the Leonardo Di Vinci kind of painter!) and a sensational Musician! Caspar is as versatile as a Swiss army knife, and like a Swiss army knife, each ability is as sharp and practical as you'd expect....Caspar McCloud is truly a man born to inherit the title "artist'...." —Steven Nagle, Editor, Rock of Ages Magazine London England

"...in years to come people will mention these names together. Ken Tamplin, Glenn Kaiser, Phil Keagy, Bob Hartman and Caspar Mc Cloud. An honor that most modern day guitar players will never even come close to getting." —Jeff Hauser, Hands in Motion Ministry

Internet Links

(1) TBN Documentary – Caspar McCloud's testimony put on National TV in the USA. - http://www.youtube.com/watch?v=-XmGqBoc0EQ – Duration approx 10 minutes.

(2) Article in regional press, Georgia, USA - http://canton-ga.patch.com/articles/canton-pastor-doubles-as-shepherd-and-rocker

(3) Further article in Cherokee Tribune – 2 churches mingle into one, one led by rocker-turned-pastor, Caspar McCloud - http://cherokeetribune.com/bookmark/14889562/article-Two+churches+partner++to+share+space+message#.TjQJ4SMLaWk.gmail

(4) Three – the official website - http://www.theministryofthree.com

(5) Caspar McCloud Ministries Inc - http://96.0.128.59/Caspar/media/media.php

(6) Video about Caspar's book "What Was I Thinking?" - http://www.youtube.com/watch?v=EN9SzIHo3Rc

Live Video Links:

(1) http://www.youtube.com/watch?v=XYbnSPjon8U &feature=related (Performing "I Love The Church")

(2) http://www.youtube.com/watch?v=-OTf8u-cB8E&feature=related (Performing "Backslider")

(3) http://www.youtube.com/watch?v=fjwxw9en3Tg (Caspar leads worship on Atlanta Channel 57)

(4) http://www.youtube.com/watch?v=as5HyAPzwu k&feature=related (Caspar on Christian TV show "Atlanta Live" (Part 1)

(5) http://www.youtube.com/watch?v=OXBHf84xTc 4&feature=related (Caspar on Christian TV show "Atlanta Live" (Part 2)

(6) http://www.youtube.com/watch?v=bsLQu4MS8Yg &feature=related Performing "Make Way" live on Atlanta Channel 57

(7) http://www.youtube.com/watch?v=PraVSprTkFo& feature=related (Performing "Holy Love")

(8) http://www.youtube.com/watch?v=wIquu9ce_ OM&feature=related (Performing "A Night In The Holy Land)

(9) http://www.youtube.com/watch?v=65Qjaddo2tM &feature=related (Performing "Help My Unbelief")

"Caspar McCloud is a really great guitarist with more of the legitimate rock and roll edge that I never had. He is also a devoted husband and father, which to me is even more important then the fact that he is such an excellent songwriter, singer and guitarist and a very gifted painter and I don't mean house painter- I mean a Di Vinci kind of painter." —Phil Keaggy

Books Offered

Nothing Is Impossible

Summary: Caspar McCloud's life story, testimony and amazing insights into the healing power of God at work today.
ISBN: 0-9754305-4-8
Barcode: 9-780975430545-90000
Release Date: 2006
Publisher: Praxis Press

What Was I Thinking?

By Caspar McCloud and Linda Lange

Summary: Reveals links between the functions of the brain, your spirit, your physical and emotional health.
ISBN: 0768432634/9780768432633
Release Date: 2010
Publisher: Destiny Image

For music CD's and DVDs visit us at:
www.theministryofthree.com

Contact Information

www.pastorcaspar@gmail.com
Facebook: Caspar McCloud Ministries

Caspar McCloud Ministries on Face Book

The Upper Room Fellowship

Caspar McCloud Senior Pastor
415 Charles Cox Drive
Canton, Georgia 30115
USA

email: pastorcaspar@gmail.com
770-475-5501

Tour Representative

Holyfire Christian Talent Agency

Steven Nagle, Director, Website:
www. Holyfiretalentagency.com
93 Allington Drive,
Email: holyfireagency@yahoo.co.uk
Strood, Rochester, Kent, ME2 3SZ.

Published by: LAMP
P.O. Box 165
Mt. Aukum, CA 95656
(530) 620-4641
lamp@truthfrees.org